For my three sons

THE BOOK OF FLOWERS

CATHERINE DONZEL

TRANSLATED FROM THE FRENCH BY DEKE DUSINBERRE

Flammarion

Paris - New York

c o n t e n t s

Editorial Director
GHISLAINE BAVOILLOT

Artistic Director
MARC WALTER

Typesetting
Bela Vista

Photoengraving
Colorscan, France

Original published in French
under the title *Le Livre des Fleurs*
Copyright 1997 © Flammarion,
Paris

Translated from the French by
Deke Dusinberre
Edited by Kate Swainson

Flammarion
26 rue Racine
75006 Paris

ISBN: 2-08013-655-0
Numéro d'édition: FA365501
Dépôt légal: July 1998
Printed and bound by
G. Canale & Co. SpA,
Borgo Torinese

Printed in Italy

CIP data may be found on page 224.

Flowers
Everywhere

Not everyone has the same taste in flowers. Yet everyone gives and receives them from time to time—a bouquet to show appreciation for services rendered, some roses in thanks for a dinner invitation, violets as a sign of friendship, lilacs to suggest budding love, floral arrangements for festive occasions. Giving flowers is not only the most popular way to express a desire to please, it is the surest way to succeed. What other gift is so likely to be understood and appreciated in even the most sensitive circumstances? Therein lies the true virtue—and perhaps power—of flowers.

A pretty bouquet can say it all—congratulations and condolences, appreciation and respect, or deep attachment and true affection extending as far as love, for which flowers are known to work wonders. When it comes to love, flowers are no small affair. As Valentine's Day approaches,

hordes of lovers are stirred and armies of florists storm flower markets in every major city. In the United States, more flowers are offered on Valentine's Day than at any other time. This trend is less marked in Europe, notably France, but does not mean that French lovers have lost their reputation! According to a 1997 survey, more than half the French give Valentine flowers to loved ones. Some florists even assert that certain Frenchmen buy *two* bouquets for the occasion—a statistical oddity that passes without comment, for discretion is a golden rule in flower shops, just as it is in the confessional.

Women, meanwhile, are delighted by a gift of flowers, claiming to prefer it to any other present, far ahead of dainty lingerie or chocolate. Not only are women the first to receive flowers, they are the first to buy them. They offer flowers on all the requisite

Nothing seduces a French woman as successfully as a bouquet, even one bought at a market stall, as witnessed by this 1950 photograph, *Lovers with Leeks*, by Robert Doisneau (*right*). *Above:* In the United States, a slightly different custom formerly required a young man to offer his date a corsage before taking her to a ball, the theater, or even the movies—illustrated here by Norman Rockwell's *After the Prom* (1957). *Previous pages:* Garden roses from the Moulié flower shop in Paris; a bouquet of old-fashioned roses wrapped in tissue paper; Marlene Dietrich being offered a heart of roses in *The Flame of New Orleans* (1941); and the bridal bouquet carried by G.

occasions, often to other women, yet also to men, who no longer take exception to such practices, except perhaps in certain Latin countries. Above all, however, women buy flowers for themselves, for their home; questions of etiquette or seduction give way to domestic considerations.

Such considerations go back a long way. In nineteenth-century Paris, flower girls strolled through the streets crying, "Flowers for you, Ladies, flowers for you." And manuals of household management urged, "Fill the home with flowers and greenery, which sanitize the dwelling. Nothing embellishes a house better than this fresh, varied finery. It is the most charming of luxuries, the highest elegance." In short, these exhortations have spurred generations of European women to "treat themselves to flowers," thanks to weekly street markets which encourage impulse-buying: it is hard to resist the wild daffodils sold on street corners, the large dahlias displayed by greengrocers, or the first clutch of peonies, all of which slip easily into a wicker shopping basket alongside pink rhubarb and green spring onions. Women generally

indulge only in the colorful, fragrant temptations of the market, where household bouquets are reasonably priced—a visit to a real florist is rarely required. No one, however, is safe from an occasional "whim." The attraction of delightful shop displays leads certain women—and men—into a minor vice which sometimes becomes a costly passion. Such extravagance, though, is rarely what it was in the days when actress Sarah Bernhardt made the fortune of Parisian florists by lining her evening lingerie with Parma violets and braiding her waist with orchids.

An irresistible desire for flowers need not be accompanied by extravagant expenditure, however. In an interview in Plinio Apuleyo Mendoza's *Fragrance of Guava*, Gabriel Garcia Marquez claimed that he only felt truly secure when surrounded by yellow flowers. It is consequently impossible for him to write without a rose—yellow, obviously—on his desk. When his writing is "not getting anywhere... [he] shout[s] for a flower!" Hence flowers—even a single, modest one—can clearly lead to excess, even among less impassioned individuals. In 1996, the British press

Autumn Flowers by Eugène-Henri Cauchois (1850–1911) (*above*). *Right: Coco* photographed by Jacques-Henri Lartigue, 1924. French novelist Colette was an unabashed picker of flowers who could never resist making up a bouquet. Her 1937 short story, *Bella-Vista*, describes the heroine gathering spring flowers as she crosses a small abandoned garden: "I encountered white arum lilies, red roses, hundreds of pointed little tulips, purple irises, and pittosporums whose fragrance makes you wonderfully drowsy. I was ruthless with the mimosa, which flowers all year round. Then with a lavish gesture I tossed my sheaf of flowers into the car."

reported the story of a very proper lady who picked a fine carnation that caught her eye in a public park. This ordinary citizen, in short, suddenly succumbed to temptation like Eve in the Garden of Eden—and wound up spending a day in jail! Not all floral indulgences are permitted. When a bouquet is obtained by *picking* flowers, there looms the vast horizon of prohibited flowerbeds and forbidden blossoms. This is a landscape that children—especially little urbanites—know well. Many of them learn the rudiments of floral art by snitching a rose or two from city gardens. Others race across the forbidden lawns of Parisian parks, braving the strident whistle of the park guard, to swipe some daisies for mother.

Diminutive thieves rarely forget their first offerings, their first thrills. Simone de Beauvoir wrote in her *Memoirs of a Dutiful Daughter* that, as a child, "touching the flowers in the park was a crime." And Agatha Christie recounted in her autobiography how, as a little girl, she was once caught picking daffodils in a neighbor's yard. Years later, she still trembled at the recollection.

Picking flowers need not always be traumatic. It can even be delightful, when vacations lead to wild fields thick with summer flowers. Yet even here, caution is required: one mustn't touch protected species such as martagon lilies, tiny wild orchids, and rare wild tulips. That leaves veronicas, buttercups, red clover, sprigs of sage, daisies, and scabious—in short, plenty to fill a vase abundantly and charmingly.

There is also enough to concoct wreaths of clematis and posies of convolvulus for little five-year-old brides, to make cute arrangements for a dolls' dinner party, and to flaunt "witches fingers" by sliding tubular foxgloves over the finger. Children's games with flowers not only reflect adult floral habits, they also create other, more

mysterious uses thanks to that "eerie" state described by Lewis Carroll in *Sylvie and Bruno*, where the young hero ceremoniously sits on a dead mouse and begins to make music with "a cluster of hare-bells" (i.e., English bluebells).

Clusters of flowers—whether cultivated or wild, purchased or picked—clearly seem to be indispensable to people everywhere. Like the air we breathe, they appear to be a kind of natural, universal necessity.

And yet there exist regions of the world where flowering plants, however beautiful, stimulate no interest, no ritual, no art.

Angelo Rossi's watercolor, painted around 1862, shows how a lady's pretty hat would be bedecked with summer blossoms (*above*). At the turn of the twentieth century, reveries and memories of flowers were strongly linked to the universe of women, including tender maternal images. *Left: Emmy and Kitty Tutzing*, resting after gathering roses in a Bavarian garden. Autochrome photo by Frank Eugène, dated 1907.

ACQUIRING THE LUXURIOUS TASTE
FOR FLOWERS

A Parisian fashion designer, highly enamored of flowers and expert in the art of flower arranging, recounted an anecdote proving that floral passions are not universal. She quite naturally indicated to an African friend who sought to please her that a gift of flowers would be most appreciated. Yet to her surprise, he found the idea astonishing: "How dreadful, my dear—a few dead twigs in some stagnant water!" It might be mentioned in passing that Victor Hugo expressed a similar attitude when he argued, in a killing phrase, that even the most charming floral composition was ultimately "a bouquet of death throes"; all civilizations that indulge abundantly in flowers feel moved by a dying bloom, yet do not necessarily reject it. The African's reaction was different, for he was indignant at the idea of making a gift of a bouquet, which he saw as a perishable object of doubtful necessity.

Indeed, Black African civilizations have little regard for flowers, a strange anthropological fact noted by Jack Goody in his fascinating book, *The Culture of Flowers*. African peoples have no tradition of cultivating flowers or adorning their bodies with them, or of offering them to gods or fellow humans. Nor do they embellish their homes with flowers. It should be pointed out that traditional African dwellings have minimal furnishing, and are therefore not very conducive to floral decoration—with nothing on which they could be conveniently placed, flowers have no room for expression. This practical detail assumes greater significance when it is realized that domestic bouquets became common in Europe only once tables, sideboards, and pedestal tables appeared in houses in the seventeenth century. This difficulty, of course, could be sidestepped by simply strewing flowers on the ground, as is done in other cultures. Furthermore, there was always the possibility of weaving wreaths and garlands of wild flowers in the absence of cultivated flowers. Yet Africa's vast tropical forest, although lush, strikingly lacks flowers. Nor is the savannah much more generous. Flowers blossom during the rainy season, only to wither immediately. When nature offers so little in the way of flowers, it is easy to see why humans show little interest.

Yet even this obvious correlation does not explain everything. There are other regions of the world where flowers abound but still spark no interest, notably the Amazonian rainforest where orchids cascade down the vines of trees to total indifference. Certain native South Americans do occasionally wear a flower behind the ear—like a grocer with his pencil—but things rarely go much farther than that.

In short, even though Africa is short of flowers and the Amazon long in them, the same attitude recurs. The abundance or lack of wild flowers is therefore not enough to explain the origin of floral customs. What, then, is the explanation for

The African continent is not completely devoid of floral customs. In North Africa, jasmine is woven into necklaces or small clusters that men stick behind an ear, while roses are appreciated along the coast of East Africa. Such customs are indebted to Islam, and exist in identical form on the Arabian peninsula. Yet in southern Arabia, bedouin tribes perpetuate floral traditions much older than Islam: bedouin men (*above*), highly conscious of their appearance, crown themselves with wild artemesia, rue, and basil or jasmine, as well as marigolds that they buy at the market.

Western ardor for gathering everything that spontaneously flowers in fields, meadows, and hedgerows? It would be wrong to think that a special sensibility enables certain cultures to appreciate floral beauty whereas others ignore it. Nothing is less natural than a taste for flowers, which in reality requires a long apprenticeship. In fact, floral passion began with cultivated flowers—it was only a ricochet effect that taught us to appreciate the special charms of wild species.

Societies that now make greatest use of cut flowers are precisely those which successfully practiced the art and science of gardening. Europe mastered the techniques very quickly, but Asia divined such secrets much earlier, and with unrivaled virtuosity. By various twists of fate,

neither Black Africa nor the Amazon could offer themselves the luxury of cultivating flowers. Indeed, flowers represent the height of luxury, since picking them means forsaking the fruit that, by nature, they herald.

They therefore become an end in themselves, their only value being the delight they provide, just like perfume, ointments, jewelry, rare foods, costly spices, silks, and embroidered fabrics. Obviously, enough surplus wealth must exist for certain people to enjoy all these sophisticated pleasures at their leisure.

The Eurasian continent, of course, boasted a wealth of temples, palaces, and prosperous towns. And everywhere, a taste for luxury blossomed into a taste for flowers.

In Japan, the annual flowering of cherry trees is a national event—the media comment daily on the imminent blossoming of the spring-time flower. Festivities then take place throughout the country, as in Kyoto (*above*), where cherry blossom has been celebrated since the sixteenth century. Processions, picnics, and tea ceremonies take place underneath the flowering branches, while poems, prints, and watercolors immortalize these graceful fruit trees.

BOUQUETS EAST AND WEST

From Western shores to the Far East, the role and arrangement of flowers assume forms as varied as the flowers themselves. In Beirut, a little handkerchief full of jasmine is given as a token of esteem when friends part. In India, bowls of white lotus petals adorn Buddhist temples, and garlands of marigolds bedeck Hindu deities. Gold tiaras braided with flowers are worn by dancers in Bali, while the Japanese eagerly await and celebrate the blossoming of cherry orchards each spring. This variety of rituals and customs nevertheless follows the outlines of a floral geography based on the fact that some peoples use only blossoms, while others place more emphasis on the beauty and length of stems.

The strange question of stems and the judgment of their ideal length is an original feature of Western bouquets. Obviously, bouquets are also supposed to have a profusion of flowers, and are all the more appreciated when generously endowed. Stems nevertheless remain a key concern in the West, for they must be long enough for the whole bouquet to bloom gracefully. Greenhouse experiments are conducted to ascertain the line, elegance, and ability of a stem to bear its

flower without bending or breaking. Of equal concern is the harmonious deployment of leaves on the stem—if the top ones are situated too high, they hide the bud; too low, they leave the corolla naked, sadly hanging in the air. Assuming stems are slender, elegant, and above all long, they can determine the price of a flower every bit as much as the bloom itself. The luxuriousness of Lachaume, the famous florist on Rue Royal in Paris, can be measured by the gigantic dimensions of the stems on display—nearly five feet high! This standard has become the chic yardstick of upmarket florists to such an extent that "lachaume flower" is used as a common noun throughout the world to indicate a flower with particularly fine proportions.

The West is not the only region of the world to take the measure of flowers. Japan, also known for cultivating the art of flower arrangement, has felt the same urge. Japan's brilliantly balanced floral compositions are precisely based on the length of stems and branches, the way that they bend,

This early twentieth-century engraving (*top*) illustrates the Japanese art of flower arranging, which became part of every young girl's education. The art, called *ikebana*, originated back in the sixteenth century among Japanese tea masters, who used flowers and greenery as part of the tea ceremony, codifying the various ways of arranging them on a tray or in a vase into "schools." *Left:* This photograph by Boubat shows that the Japanese express their love of flowers in many ways, such as this child kneeling beneath a shower of petals. *Above:* On the other side of the planet, a display at Lachaume's in Paris symbolizes the Western spirit of floral art—dense clusters of lush peonies and handsome lilies on long stems.

intersect, and mirror one another. The comparison ends there, however. Japanese bouquets are entirely different from their Western counterparts. Flowers are few and far between, and occasionally absent. The profusion of flowers so appreciated in the West was deprecated back in 1906 by Kakuzo Okakura, an ardent defender of Japanese traditions, in his *Book of Tea*: "The wanton waste of flowers among Western communities is... appalling. The number of flowers cut daily to adorn the ballrooms and banquet tables of Europe and America, to be thrown away on the morrow, must be something enormous; if strung together they might garland a continent... Whither do they all go, these flowers, when the revelry is over?

Nothing is more pitiful than to see a faded flower remorselessly flung upon a dung heap."

As a discerning thinker concerned by the sad destiny of cut flowers, Okakura was equally worried about their fate at the hands of his own compatriots. He felt that Japanese customs—more thoughtful, more economical—were less open to criticism than Western excesses. Yet he made no attempt to disguise the dread behavior of the Flower Master, that highly venerated artist who strolled up and down the emperor's garden "armed with scissors and a tiny saw," cutting, bending, twisting flowers into impossible positions, imposing on them a diet of "salt, vinegar, alum, and sometimes vitriol," or even burning

In certain regions of southern India, every day begins with flowers. The blessing of the gods is obtained by ritually arranging flowers on the doorstep (*above*), a composition that disperses as the day progresses. *Right:* Many other countries and civilizations also observe floral rites, such as Popayan, Colombia, where Easter week is celebrated among countless flowers. The color changes each day of the week, becoming completely white at the end of the celebrations. During processions, each float is preceded by a *sahumadora*, or girl carrying flowers and incense. Such girls are an eternal symbol of youth and prosperity.

them with "red-hot coals" to prevent the sap from escaping.

Chinese bouquets, although far removed from Western customs, are also part of the "long stem" realm. Here, however, the stems are woody, being branches of peach or orange trees or peony bushes, which are preferred over herbaceous flowers. For that matter, bouquets are rather rare in a land that so adores potted plants. Bouquets nevertheless make a brief appearance during New Year celebrations, when they blossom in every home: a flowering branch—a promise of future happiness—is carefully placed in a vase whose importance is as great as its contents. In China, the precious New Year vase is a treasured family heirloom.

All bouquet civilizations conjugate their passion for flowers with beautiful vases of fine porcelain, clear crystal, highly colored ceramics, or dark pewter. Yet vases suddenly lose all their importance—and their usefulness—when we enter southern Asia. Stems, of no interest here, are tossed to the winds. Only blossoms are kept. In markets in Delhi and Bombay, flowers are sold in bulk, by weight, from huge mounds of red rosebuds and dazzling marigold heads. Some merchants braid these blossoms with twists of fine bark, thereby entering the realm of garlands, which stretches beyond India to southeast Asia and even Polynesia.

The propagation of all forms of floral expression—whether favoring stems, blossoms, or both—reflects the rise of certain civilizations and their global domination. As the West increasingly influences international taste, Western-style bouquets have begun appearing everywhere, even where they were once unknown. This means that Hong Kong, like the United States, now celebrates Valentine's Day with an avalanche of roses imported for the occasion from Holland. In warm weather, rich Chinese have large bunches of sweet peas flown in from Paris greenhouses. The same thing is happening in Tokyo, where a gift of flowers would have seemed incongruous not so very long ago; the Japanese now consider bringing a bouquet when making courtesy calls (traditionally an occasion for offering delicacies).

Things have thus come full circle. In the late nineteenth century, the Western concept of the bouquet was transformed by the discovery of Japanese floral art. Now it is Japan's turn to learn about spontaneity and naturalness from Western florists. The world of flowers is a continual flow of exchanges.

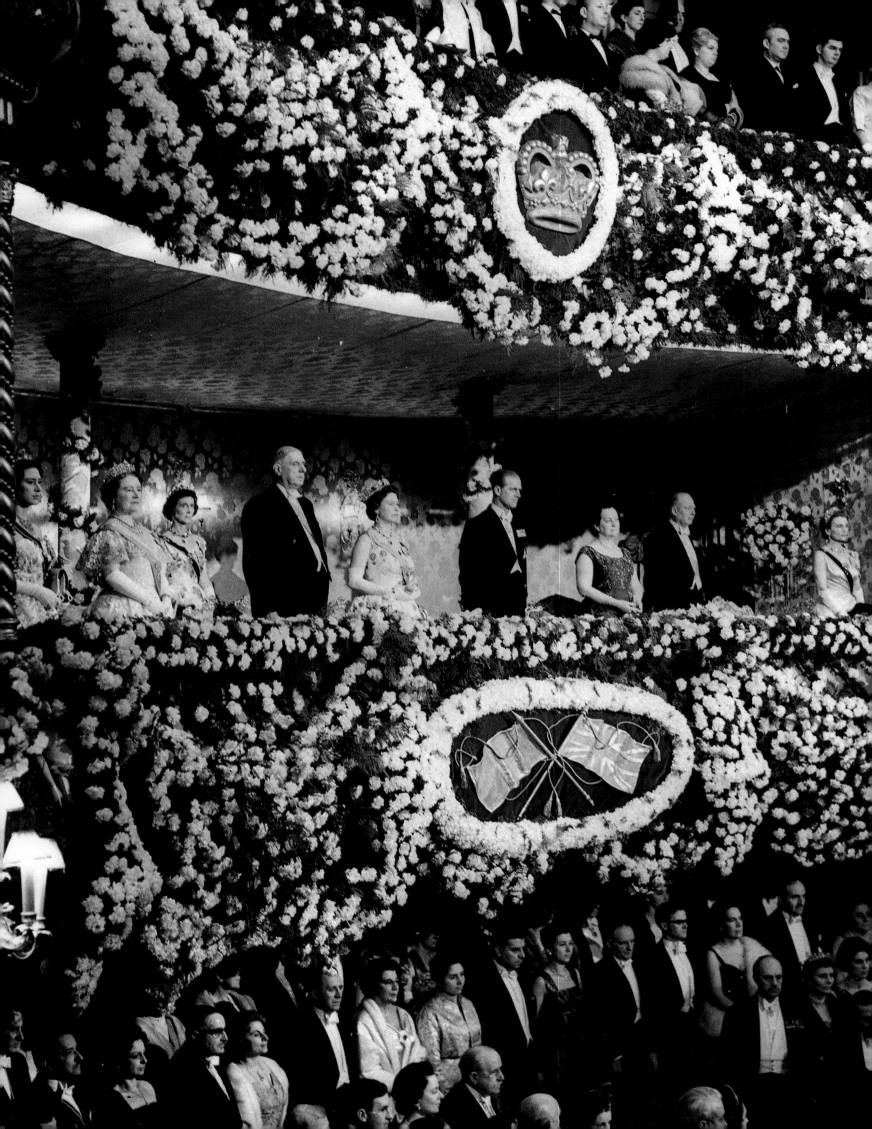

From Buckingham's Carnations
to Atlanta's Sunflowers

It would be a mistake to think that the internationalization of Western bouquets means they are becoming standardized. Their very region of origin—Europe and the United States—presents a veritable mosaic of attitudes and customs. This can be seen in the diversity of floral purchases, which vary enormously in quantity from one country to another. At the top of the list come Switzerland and Austria, where flowers are consumed plentifully. They are rivaled only by Norway, which also indulges in flowers shamelessly—its long northern winters encourage floral decoration in the warm glow of candles and brightly colored interiors. The Dutch also rank high. Their love of bouquets dates back centuries and they are the world's leading producer of flowers. France, meanwhile, comes far behind Germany, Belgium, and Italy, but ahead of the United States and Britain. The latter are outdistanced by almost all Western countries—it is hard to understand why the British, who are so enamored of flowers, buy so few. It might be supposed that their small back gardens (attached to almost all urban townhouses, not to mention country cottages) provide an inexpensive source of flowers, making florists redundant. The Queen, after all, sets the tone: whereas flower arrangers at France's presidential palace go to a large wholesale market south of Paris to make regular

purchases, those at Buckingham Palace simply head out to the garden with scissors. Extravagant floral expenditures are avoided—for official banquets in the ballroom at Buckingham, the Queen usually asks for a cascade of red and yellow carnations to harmonize with the gold plate, the scarlet and purple chairs, and the throne canopy—all picked from the gardens at Windsor. It is a question both of home economics and national temperament.

The endless subtleties behind flowers can never be fully grasped. Without access to innermost feelings, it is impossible to know why Germans never offer a bouquet without having first removed the paper in which it is wrapped; or why the French are always careful to present flowers in odd numbers; or why bouquets in Spain and Italy are fuzzier, larger, mistier than elsewhere. Nor can anyone explain why fashions suddenly erupt—sunflowers invading the Olympic Games in Atlanta and adorning all the victors—or why certain colors become all the rage.

It is a fair guess that this constant diversity in tastes and attitudes has been with us throughout history. The origin of Western bouquets as they emerged in old Europe is rich with exuberant if passing infatuations, sudden disaffections, and customs as capricious as they were fleeting. The enormous success of contemporary floral art, then, is just another stage in a dramatic story in which everything blossoms again and again—flowers, fashions, feelings.

Sarah Ferguson's daughters at the wedding of former nanny Alison Wordley (*above*) hold a typically British hoop of flowers. *Left:* Covent Garden Opera House, magnificently decorated for an official state visit by Charles de Gaulle. For weddings and major events, the Queen and her entourage turn to good London florists, some of whom have been supplying the court since Victorian days (Lady Diana's famous bouquet was ordered from Longman's, a firm founded in London in 1896). Members of the royal family nevertheless generally content themselves with flowers picked by gardeners at Windsor Castle. The same is true of the Queen's subjects, two-thirds of whom never buy bouquets, relying exclusively on their own gardens.

Garlanded, Wreathed, and Strewn

Floral fashions follow one another, forgetting one another in no time at all. Our immediate forebears, of course, bequeathed us a few orange flowers under glass and countless photo albums showing brides wearing wreaths and holding bouquets, ladies sporting wide-brimmed hats bedecked with flowers, banquets featuring vast floral arrangements, and interiors revealing everyday flowers in vases and baskets. These images provide a glimpse of trends and passing fancies for certain blooms or arrangements. Yet things are murkier when it comes to customs governing the giving of bouquets, or the various ways in which men were supposed to fill their buttonhole. Less than one hundred years ago, floral savoir-faire entailed a whole range of rules, almost none of which have survived. The very awareness that they once existed is even being lost.

Strangely, although collective memory of flowers has faded in less than a century, it often remains extraordinarily sharp when focused on certain images that probably shaped floral passions over two thousand years ago. Just mention the pomp of imperial Rome and everyone pictures parades of triumphant legions showered with petals, generals wreathed in laurel, marble palaces carpeted in flowers, and divine statues festooned with roses. The extreme lavishness with which Rome bedecked itself in flowers entranced the West, which has never been the same. Western art endlessly depicted these mounds of garlands and wreaths in eighteenth-century mythological paintings, followed in the nineteenth century by kitsch canvases of beautiful Roman women draped in flowers (notably painted by Sir Lawrence Alma-Tadema). Then came Hollywood where, from superproductions to modest B-pictures, slaves strewed petals everywhere in order to render anachronistic cardboard sets more authentic.

What makes antiquity's floral sensuousness so fascinating, however, is not just the image but the

The garlands and crowns of Athens and Rome, illustrated in frescoes and bas-reliefs, were a constant source of inspiration and reverie for the West. Thus the poet Sappho (7th–6th century B.C.E.) wrote: "And you, my Dika, crown your lovely locks with garlands,/twining shoots of anise in your tender hands,/for the blessed Graces come the sooner to those adorned/with flowers, and turn away from the ungarlanded." *Left: Spring* by Sir Lawrence Alma-Tadema, 1894. *Above: Summer* by Sir William Ernest Reynold, 1862. *Previous pages:* Detail of Alma-Tadema's *Spring* (left), and detail of a frieze from Empress Joséphine's chateau in Malmaison, France, early nineteenth century (right).

objective reality of it. We yearn to know what the famous rose of Paestum, used by the ancients, must have looked like. Similarly, Western imagination is stirred by the vanished splendors of the seven wonders of the world, with a special sense of loss for the Hanging Gardens—a magnificent terraced park, irrigated at grand expense, whose exotic species towered above the rooftops of Babylon. Long before the rise of Rome, in fact, the Middle East was known for its skillful gardening, taste for decorative plants and, later, a specific attraction to flowers. Peoples of the Fertile Crescent stressed floral gracefulness in friezes delicately carved with rosettes, palm fronds, and lotus flowers. This same lotus, blue or white, also flowered in the cool pools of the Nile. Lotuses were cherished in pharaonic Egypt, and were carved into the capitals of temple columns, sometimes in the form of a single bud, sometimes in beribboned bunches.

The purity and naturalness of these architectural bouquets suggests that Egyptians were not only expert builders and gardeners but also wonderful florists. Both Greeks and Romans, for that matter, praised the subtleties of Egyptian floral art. Celebrations during the New Kingdom—one of the most refined periods of Egyptian history—featured bouquets of poppies, daisies, cornflowers, and lotuses, which were also woven into ladies' hair.

Elegant and seductive Egyptian women were fully aware of the power of flowers, deploying all their charms. Much later, Cleopatra was still clearly conversant in this art. It was Caesar, first of all, whom she smothered in flowers. During a splendid banquet she gave on his arrival in Alexandria, all the guests were crowned with roses whose fragrance blended with the heady scent of spikenard. She then repeated the act with Mark Antony, giving magnificent banquets in his honor, strewing rose petals two-feet deep on the marble floor (held in place by an invisible net). Antony was completely won over, yet unable to help Cleopatra achieve her dream of a grand Eastern empire. Egypt, at any rate, had long ago lost its soul by abandoning the beautiful Nile lotus in favor of the rose, that foreign flower imported by the armies of Alexander the Great.

LOVERS' WREATHS
IN ANCIENT GREECE

The Greeks introduced roses wherever the mild climate permitted, in colonies such as Massilia, Nike, and Antipolis (the modern cities of Marseille, Nice, and Antibes, whose floral reputations are therefore far from recent). The Greeks probably grew *Rosa gallica*, thought to be the oldest variety cultivated in Europe, lightly scented and with a double corolla. Whatever the case, these roses were obviously most exquisite, being dedicated to Aphrodite and to affectionate demonstrations of love. In addition to roses, Greeks also liked to grow and pick narcissus, marjoram, and stock, not to mention their penchant for violets (the emblem of Athens).

Greece had always appreciated ornaments of vegetation, although originally this meant leafy greenery. Eastern expeditions soon corrupted that simplicity, especially through contact with Egypt and its seductive floral compositions. Athenians then began weaving blossoms into wreaths and garlands (which remained the primary forms of Western floral expression until the Renaissance). The first to benefit from these new ornaments were the gods—lilies decorated the statues of Artemis, red poppies adorned Morpheus, and numerous flowers strewed the altar of Zeus, who loved them all.

What was good enough for the gods was soon good enough for mortals. The Eastern custom of bedecking banquets with flowers was also swiftly adopted. Prior to a repast, slaves would braid wreaths for all the guests, bringing new ones as soon as the originals began to wilt. The sweet scent and freshness of flowers were supposed to enhance the pleasure of socializing. Yet these fragile crowns had other, more prosaic virtues: medical treatises claimed that a band of flowers worn tightly around the head could forestall the undesirable effects of wine. Not all plants were suitable, however—a wreath of stock and marjoram inevitably produced a migraine, while one of narcissus might lead to an attack of nerves. Ivy, however, being one of the attributes of Dionysus, worked wonders, especially when combined with violets, since it dissipated "heavy-headedness" as successfully as roses which, of course, were also welcome. The petals of roses braided around drinking vessels were

even scattered in the wine, leading to the practice of *coronas bibere* ("drinking the crown").

Flowers, so clearly associated with the delights and pleasures of life, ultimately accompanied many public and private events. Wreaths were worn by victors, heads of official missions, orators, passengers on departing ships, and by the ships themselves. Wreaths were also awarded to great men, just as grateful countries now award their citizens medals and decorations. And, of course, wreaths were exchanged passionately and tenderly by lovers, who tried to read omens into them. The color of flowers might confirm a rendezvous; the way the petals scattered and fell from the head-dress might dash all hopes or encourage bold moves. Yet no promise was more erotic than the sending of a wilted wreath worn by a woman the previous evening, to which were added several apples from which a bite had been taken. Because such gifts were inexpensive, however, a feeble affair would be described as "loving with apples and roses." True conviction required more effort. And a spurned lover who hoped to regain favor had to open his pocket-book, decorating the door of his indifferent lady with many highly sophisticated and preferably costly garlands.

Greek moralists and polemicists criticized all these wreaths as evidence of a dangerous trend toward ostentation, lavishness, extravagant expenditure, and lascivious pleasures. The philosopher Theophrastus (whose *Characters* inspired seventeenth-century moralists like La Bruyère), described an official who damaged votive altars by heaping them with so many garlands, and who always appeared in town with magnificent blossoms on his brow.

Such excessive vanity bordered on silliness. It could hardly compare, however, with the floral extravagance that Rome never managed—despite warnings by the wise—to control.

Flower stalls and markets already existed in ancient Greece, for a certain skill was needed to produce all the wonderfully flirtatious wreaths evoked in the 1866 painting by American artist John Lafarge, *Greek Love Token* (*above*). Some female merchants in antiquity—the trade being essentially feminine—became famous. Glykera, a weaver of garlands, became the first florist to go down in history thanks to the painter Pausias, who fell madly in love with her. He reportedly exhausted himself trying to paint the floral compositions of his mistress, who challenged him by constantly modifying them.

SHOWERS OF ROSES IN ROME

By the age of Augustus (63 B.C.E.–14 C.E.), Romans were growing flowers in the courtyards of city homes, where frescoes of gladioli, daisies, lilies, crocus, and myrtle extended the space of little gardens. Under shaded porticoes, Romans enjoyed the delightful coolness of flowered groves and probably picked the blossoms that adorned domestic altars. Yet that was not enough. Even in the last days of the republic, a lavish lifestyle was led by the rich and famous, especially at Pompeii and Herculaneum, where Romans built summer residences and indulged in idle display of precious fabrics, jewels, ointments, spices, and—obviously—flowers. Horticulture boomed on the seaside plain of Campania, whose volcanic soil remains so fertile to this day. Supplying large towns with flowers was a lucrative business, stimulating enterprising growers who

already employed hothouses, forcing flowers by watering with them lukewarm water. Growers could thus continue supplying the market right up to the first heavy frosts, at which point Egypt took over—the so-called "Alexandrian" fleet docked twice a month at Ostia (then the port of Rome), laden with all kinds of flowers. Not everyone approved of these spiraling imports, as pointless as they were costly. Nor did everyone appreciate the fact that the fertile grain fields of Campania were being given over to flowers. Once again, as in ancient Greece, polemics and diatribes mounted, but to no avail.

The rest of the story is well known, its heroes remaining notorious if not glorious. First there was Nero, known for his violent excesses, which were always accompanied by masses of flowers: petals had to be strewn when he walked along the beach not far from Naples where he had once tried to drown his mother; countless wreaths were presumably required for his numerous weddings; and he is credited with inaugurating the famous "showers of roses." These showers—a show of floral magic—were just one of the wonders of the Golden House he built on the Esquiline Hill. In the round dining room which rotated night and day to imitate the movement of the earth, ivory panels in the ceiling opened to release flowers and fragrances that seemed to fall from the sky. The cost was astronomical, but the fashion caught on. Some 150 years later, another notorious emperor, Heliogabalus, went even further. His shower of petals became an endless flood, transforming the show into tragedy. Three canopy-loads of petals were unleashed one after another, tumbling down into the banquet hall. The effect was stunning, indeed breathtaking—several guests had just enough time to applaud before they suffocated to death under the roses.

In a way, Rome's extravagant passion for roses contained the seeds of their downfall. The exquisitely beautiful Roman rose was the flower not only of life and love but also—due to its fleetingness—of funerals. It would rise again, almost as a warning, in eighteenth-century "vanity" still lifes, which symbolically evoked the fleeting, inconsequential nature of human existence.

Until then, however, Rome's fall carried everything with it—the West lost its taste for flowers, its botanical knowledge, and perhaps even a certain idea of happiness. All of which awaited rediscovery.

A pretty basket of flowers, from a second-century mosaic (*above*). *Right:* Detail from Alma-Tadema's *Roses of Heliogabalus*. The charming idea of a shower of roses, launched by Nero, took quite another turn with the Emperor Heliogabalus. His guests—accustomed to his cruel jokes, such as unleashing hungry tigers in the middle of a banquet—were relieved the day the fragrant "rain" began falling. But it fell again and again, becoming torrential. Some women covered their faces, others sought the exits—only to discover that the doors were barred by armed legionnaires. A delighted Heliogabalus watched his guests suffocate under this shroud of roses.

EARLY MIDDLE AGES:
MONASTIC FLOWERS

The centuries following the fall of Rome are often called the Dark Ages, a troubled period generally remembered for rampaging barbarian hordes who burned, pillaged, and spread terror everywhere. These invasions alone, however, cannot explain the marked decline in floral customs, even though people in the early Middle Ages were obviously keener to erect high fortifications than to dig pretty little gardens. In fact, it was the Church that deliberately trampled on what remained of Roman wreaths and garlands, in an effort to assert its authority by clearly distinguishing itself from still-thriving pagan cults. All displays of idolatry were forbidden: statues of pagan gods and offerings of flowers were stained by the memory of blood sacrifices. The congregation of Christians was therefore obliged to renounce the cult of flowers not only during religious ceremonies but also in everyday life. This prohibition was even deemed to include the picking of wild flowers, according to Clement of Alexandria, a converted pagan who became an eminent theologian. It is hard to know whether Clement's strictures were followed to the letter, but he certainly struck a heavy blow.

And yet it was the Church itself that sparked the rebirth of floral tradition which, paradoxically, it had preserved. The cultural revival accompanying Charlemagne's eighth-century empire stimulated an enthusiastic re-reading of ancient texts, notably works on botany. Botanical knowledge had progressed little—or even regressed—since the military physician Dioscorides wrote *De Materia Medica* at the end of the first century C.E. As the first illustrated treatise on botany, this text remained a key reference work right up to the Renaissance. Like other

works, it had been piously sheltered in monastic libraries, then endlessly copied by monks who thereby preserved humanity's floral knowledge.

It was also in the cloisters, moreover, that gardening techniques were perpetuated. Vegetables and aromatic herbs were grown there for the needs of the religious community. Flowers could be cultivated as well, providing they had a recognizable use; often enough, they were attributed a number medicinal virtues that justified taking an interest in them. Such interest may not always have been purely practical, however. Although not yet many varieties were cultivated during the Carolingian period, a number of charming local flowers were grown, such as marigolds, love-in-a-mist, mauves, and lilies. Nor was it necessarily a sin to marvel at the beauty of plants as a clear manifestation of divine generosity. For that matter, placing a few flowers on the altar was sometimes even tolerated—they thereby recovered some of their innocence in this strictly decorative, non-liturgical role. The significance of early ornamental tendencies should not be overstated, however. The idea that flowers should be useful—as cure or nourishment—predominated for a long time. The most elegant blossoms were primarily used for herbal infusions. Such brews were not always curative: seeds of the medicinal peony, not included in the monastic pharmacopoeia, were sometimes harvested on dark, moonless nights for their allegedly poisonous effect. Hence flowers were still suspect, still associated with obscure rites, with strange beliefs still lurking in the depths of peasant consciousness. Flowers had to be kept under close watch, had to be rescued from black magic and witchcraft.

Yet by the late eleventh century, flowers were being used as a means of communication by monks at Cluny when silence was imposed, thereby assuming the Christian mission of "bearing a

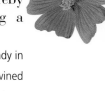

Medieval illuminated manuscripts reveal a predilection for two-color arrangements, as seen in this red-and-white wreath woven by a lady in her small garden, illustrated in a 1460 French translation of Boccaccio (*right*). The alternation of red and white flowers represents entwined symbols of her chastity and her passion for the man she loves. Perhaps she is using roses picked from the trellis behind, or carnations from the flowerbed beside her. In the foreground can be seen traditional medieval flowers such as columbine, lavender, and rosemary, used for both decorative and medicinal purposes. Wild mauve (several blossoms are scattered on this page) was also part of the medieval pharmacopoeia, being used in a "four-flower" tisane, or herbal decoction.

message." Indeed, the vast medieval world was perceived as an immense web of symbolic messages in which flowers came to play a key role. To this end they were rebaptized, under the aegis of the Virgin, whose cult rose dramatically in the eleventh century. Mary, as Queen of Heaven—and possibly also as a woman—was henceforth covered in flowers. When picking a delightful bunch for her, all varieties became "Our Lady's" flowers: convolvulus was styled "Our Lady's Nightcap," the cowslip became her "keys" and tiny wild orchids her "slippers." Behind one lady, however, another may well lurk—today those same orchids are known in French as "Venus's slippers." The attempt to Christianize flowers was thus superimposed on pagan use without entirely eliminating it. All these symbols, both pious and profane, continued to exist side by side. Since flowers say only what they are told to say, it became possible to shift from one subject to another.

MAKING CHAPLETS, STREWING FLOWERS

By the time of the first Crusades, decorative flowers were budding more boldly in cloisters, eventually breaking free of monastic enclosure to participate in the chivalrous jousting of knights and their demoiselles. In *Perceval*, the romance penned around 1180 by Chrétien de Troyes, maidens slept in rooms scented with freshly strewn flowers, their gowns woven of "white silk with golden flowers" or "purple silk dotted with silver flowers." These ladies welcomed their knights like princes, having "garlands hung from all houses, petals strewn in all streets." In the *Roman de la Rose*, meanwhile, composed in the late thirteenth century, the rose was identified with love and desire in a passionate quest that drove the poet to "approach and pluck it."

Alongside sentimental allegories, flowers were making a very real comeback in the "pleasure

The fashion for flowered hats reached its height in the thirteenth and fourteenth centuries, although it remained popular much longer among the lower classes and in religious ceremonies. In European courts, however, this fashion soon became overly sophisticated—the flowers worn by Queen Isabeau of Bavaria and her ladies-in-waiting (*above, La Cité des Dames*, 1410) were made of precious metal, set with pearls and gemstones, stitched on to their head-dresses. Shown in vignette is nigella, or "love-in-a-mist," now used in bouquets but once employed as a condiment or as a remedy against spider bites.

Starting in the fourteenth century, flowers entered the vast, cold spaces of churches and castles in woven form. There was a great vogue for tapestries in the *millefleurs* design, as seen in this early sixteenth-century Flemish tapestry of *The Three Fates* (*above*). Tapestries were used in exactly the same way as garlands and festoons of fresh flowers—they were constantly moved around, hung up and taken down, transferred from one castle to another, and even placed against facades or hung across the street during festivities and ceremonial entries by monarchs.

gardens" henceforth landscaped on lordly manors. Islam introduced the Crusaders to a new savoir-faire, and they returned from the Holy Land dazzled by all that they saw: skillful metalwork, artfully tooled and gilded leather, silk fabrics, flowered carpets, and above all the admirable gardens that Moors cultivated in the wake of conquests from Persia (with its ancient tradition of Babylonian gardens) to Spain (where Andalusia was under Arab domination from the eighth century onward). These edenic gardens were full of birds, flowers, gurgling fountains, and creaking water wheels. Several new species growing there enriched Western herbals, notably *Caryophyllus* marigolds that smelled of cloves. And the infidels' almost exclusive passion for roses would soon be shared by Christian knights.

All floral customs, sacred and secular, henceforth focused on roses, the most sophisticated and eloquent of medieval flowers. Charged with symbolism, carved in stone, and stained in glass, roses were transformed into the rose windows of vast Gothic cathedrals, representing the finest—and most monumental—tribute that a simple flower has ever received. The homage is particularly explicit in York cathedral, where the chapter house bears the inscription *"Ut rosa flos florum sic est domus domorum"* ("Just as the Rose is flower of flowers, so is this the house of houses").

Gothic roses inaugurated an early floral restoration of customs that lasted until the Renaissance, becoming one of the most delightful and pleasant periods in this history of flowers. At no other time did people adopt flowers with as much spontaneity and simple, spring-like joy. One attractive feature was the fashion for "chaplets," which were nothing other than Roman-style wreaths or crowns. They were used in more or less the Roman way, namely for celebrations, banquets, and flirtation, but also in crowned statues of the Virgin during processions where flowers henceforth proliferated freely.

Cleverly stripped of its antique connotations, a chaplet could be worn in fine weather by men as well as women. It might be composed of a hoop of wood or a roll of cloth on to which leaves and flowers were stuck. Or greenery might be braided together—watercress, for example, or mint or basil—then threaded with tiny posies. Flowers themselves were still rare, and sometimes people had to settle for "green chaplets" when roses were out of season and violets no longer bloomed.

The making of these headdresses was an innocent, pastoral activity enjoyed by ladies who lovingly concocted them while chatting in the orchard. Some women worked with a great deal of skill, or in any case a great deal of feeling, because these wreaths obviously always bore some hidden meaning. For young men sometimes joined these female gatherings, exchanging chaplets and conversation that often ended in flower fights—nothing being more flirtatious, of course, than "throwing herbs and flowers in each other's faces."

Floral headgear, so convenient near gardens and orchards, was not limited to the rural

Seraphim painted by Benozzo Gozzoli (1420–97) in this detail (*right*) from a fresco in the chapel of the Palazzo Medicis-Riccardi in Florence are preparing heavy festoons of flowers for some divine celebration. In their scarves they carry the flowers to make "chaplets" or little coronals. *Above:* The chaplets worn by angels surrounding the Virgin in this painting by the Master of the Costello Nativity (15th century) are made of roses—such garlands of roses progressively became flowers of ivory, mother-of-pearl, or coral, ultimately evolving into the precious beads still called a "rosary."

aristocracy. City noblemen prized chaplets even more. In twelfth-century Paris, the vogue spurred the founding of a chaplet-makers guild by gardeners outside the city walls who grew little plots of everything they needed to concoct head-dresses and other ornaments. Nor were interiors—at least in the finest homes—devoid of greenery and cut flowers, either garlanded or strewn on the floor.

Bouquets, however, remained rare. There was simply no furniture designed to take a vase and allow a bouquet to be leisurely appreciated—no pier or pedestal tables, indeed few permanent tables at all. Everything in a medieval apartment was moveable, no object had a permanently assigned place. This precariousness lasted into the seventeenth century (when the first notions of interior design evolved) and partly explains the rather late emergence of bouquets. Festive color generally came in the form of braids of blossoms and greenery (even shrubbery) that framed doors

and festooned walls. Such decorations were designed to last an evening, then taken down once the festivities were over. Decorative flowers were not yet in regular use, except perhaps in the case of strewing greenery on the ground. Flowers and greenery not only carpeted the floor during ceremonies, but were also used on a daily basis in bedrooms, strewn with clusters of broom or flag, or clutches of lavender or mint. These plants were generally chosen for their fragrance: they not only freshened the air and made the room more pleasant, but were valued as a prophylactic, their aromatic scent having the reputation of warding off infection and noxious vapors.

Another way of strewing flowers involved scattering petals on the tablecloth during meals. Medieval table settings were bare, disordered, and unrefined, but the cloth covering the table (thereby hiding the unmatched trestles under the plank) was of great importance. From an early

White lilies (*Lilium candidum*) were known in antiquity (*left*), and were the most prized ornamental flowers in the Middle Ages, along with roses. *Above:* Lilies were also the favorite emblem of the heavenly host, as seen in *The Coronation of the Virgin* by Filippo Lippi (1406–69). Furthermore, they were widely used as a heraldic device; a red lily figures on the coat of arms of Florence, and a gold "lily"—or *fleur-de-lys* —appeared on the banner of Clovis, king of the Franks, as early as the fifth century. In fact, the French royal *fleur-de-lys* is probably an iris. It is said that Clovis, fording the River Vienne shortly before his victory over the Visigoths, noted a large population of little yellow irises, commonly called "marsh lilies." Thanks to the similarity of the name, the flower became the heraldic emblem of the French monarchy.

date, fragrant blossoms and sprigs were scattered across it. Once again, the original motivation may not have been decorative, but rather to mask the unpleasant smell of cured meats. By 1499, however, a resolutely decorative intent is evident in Francesco Colonna's famous *Hypnerotomachia Poliphili* (*Dream of Poliphilo*). This Italian Renaissance text describes a rather unlikely meal of several courses (each one corresponding to a whole series of dishes) which, despite its exaggeration, probably contains a kernel of truth. Tablecloths and flowers were changed with each course, and Colonna describes at some length the combinations of color and materials. First the tables were covered in green silk with gold and silver fringe, strewn with violets brought by a maiden in a basket of precious metal. Then came a cloth of Persian silk covered with orange flowers; gray silk cloth was scattered with white, pink, and vermilion Damascus roses; fine yellow satin was strewn with lily-of-the-valley; crimson silk bore yellow, white, and purple stock; then came purple silk and jasmine flowers, finally followed by white linen strewn with fragrant carnations. Colonna points out that the cloths were successively shaken so that a deep carpet of multicolored blossoms spread beneath the guests' feet by the end of the meal. Afterward, sweeping the floor left it "clean and shiny like a looking glass." Strewings of fresh flowers were slowly replaced by tablecloths with embroidered floral patterns, becoming just a memory by the seventeenth century.

The charming, spring-like customs of the Gothic period slowly gave way to other habits. Soon pretty chaplets were out of fashion—the Renaissance aristocracy still wreathed itself in flowers, but only on playful occasions such as masquerades and costumed festivities. For people of rank, the standard head-dress became a felt or velvet hat that eschewed flowers in favor of ostrich feathers, gemstones, or aglets of gold or silver.

Gardens were no longer ransacked with the same casualness. Flowers that medieval Westerners had plucked by the armful, almost thoughtlessly, in order to concoct infusions or cover the floor, were henceforth carefully studied, catalogued, and labeled in herbals. Up to that point, people had never studiously gazed upon flowers. More or less consigned to a utilitarian role, flowers had never merited individual contemplation revealing their specific complexity and beauty. During the Renaissance, however—which invented both microscope and telescope—the gaze was everything. It was therefore quite natural that a new attitude to flowers would be shaped by imagery. In this sphere, the pioneering work of painters and miniaturists—who were the first to explore the minute realm of flowers—preceded botanical research by several decades.

Considerable quantities of flowers were required to fulfill floral customs in the feudal era and the Renaissance. Because of their scarcity, such flowers were costly. As a luxury item, like spices, they became part of the rent-in-kind system, which included payments of "bushels of roses." That explains the floral offering made by this elegant young man at the feet of Jesus in *The Holy Family* by Bernard van Orley (1488–1541)—the offer of jasmine, pansies, and carnations represents a precious tribute made by a vassal to his lord.

FLORAL IMAGES

Novel imagery had already taken root in fifteenth-century depictions of small bouquets, notably in paintings of the Annunciation. These were no sophisticated floral arrangements: flowers were randomly stuck in a makeshift vase such as an apothecary's jar, water ewer, or drinking glass. Furthermore, the choice of flowers indicates that the intention was above all symbolic, the prime role being awarded to the lily as an attribute of virginal purity. And yet these images are astonishingly life-like. The same concern for naturalism applied to the daisies, violets, pansies, and roses that filled the borders of illuminated manuscripts during that same period. "Real" blossoms are gracefully arrayed on the page, exactly as they must have appeared when picked and studied. The Van Eyck brothers excelled in floral studies, as did French painter Jean Bourdichon, whose illuminated books of hours featured butterflies alighting on mayflowers accurate down to the last stamen. Also worth mentioning is Jean Fouquet, who decorated the *Book of Hours of Simon de Varie* with delightfully fresh and

realistic columbine. Albrecht Dürer went still further, being the first to produce virtuoso paintings that were veritable portraits of plants and flowers.

From that point onward, the capacity to observe—and to marvel at what one saw—governed the scope of knowledge among not only painters but also botanists, who were the first to benefit from advances in painterly naturalism. The sixteenth century yielded a sudden wealth of new botanical treatises, swiftly made available

In 1542, German botanist Leonhart Fuchs published a large illustrated herbal that included over five hundred illustrations of plants and flowers. His book, *De Historia Stirpium*, provides rare images of the artists themselves, shown here attentively copying flowers from nature (*above*). They were interested in all flowers, even modest violets, which Albrecht Dürer depicted in a small bouquet in 1503 (*top*), bunched in a collar of leaves exactly as is still done by florists today. *Right:* The blue columbines with which Jean Fouquet decorated the 1455 *Book of Hours of Simon de Varie* (*top*) are as fresh as the ones picked in today's gardens (*bottom*).

through the invention of printing. Such books were henceforth based on direct study of plants, in collaboration with artists whose illustrations were sometimes more revolutionary than the text itself. All these publications nevertheless appeared halfway between pharmacopoeia and botanical text. Plants remained primarily medicinal, in deference to the ancients and especially Dioscorides, whose text was widely translated. Yet the splendid inventories illustrated by artists after patient expeditions largely helped to spur the public's curiosity, refining its taste in plants and flowers.

That taste was itself undergoing dramatic evolution, as testified by these scholarly tomes which—paradoxically—were so concerned with floral aesthetics. Daléchamps' compilation of earlier books, published in Lyon in 1587 under the title of *Histoire Générale des Plantes*, notably included a practical chapter on the beauty of flowers and their various uses. Daléchamps informed readers of the most fragrant varieties, also indicating those that "smell bad" or "wilt" too swiftly. Such advice obviously concerned cut flowers, which were beginning to appear in various bouquets destined either for the interior or "to be held in the hand and suddenly brought to the nose, to enjoy the sight and scent." Interest in this type of arrangement was apparently still a novelty insofar as Daléchamps felt that "bouquet" needed defining: "Flowers are taken by the handful and placed in painted vases or earthen pots filled with water." Although this reads more like a recipe than a description of floral artistry, the arrival of costly, foreign varieties, along with the glorification of the individual beauty of each flower, would eventually lead to more skillful arrangements.

At first, however, people were amazed and fascinated by "exotic" flowers without quite knowing what to do with them. Daléchamps predictably included a sketch of a tulip, the new flower depicted for the first time in 1561 by Swiss herborist Conrad Gesner. It left Daléchamps somewhat puzzled and uninspired, however. He classified it among the lilies, accompanied by the following description: "There is another highly beautiful plant, which some include among the red lilies, and which is called Tulipam, from the name used by the Turks in their language."

Daisies, pansies, and mauve can be distinctly recognized in the border decoration for *The Book of Hours of Engelbert of Nassau*, illuminated in Belgium around 1485 (*top*). *Left:* Some of the same varieties, as well as a small double carnation, recur on the page of a book recounting the legend of Saint Stephen. The way in which all these blooms were scattered across the margins of fifteenth-century manuscripts evokes the custom of strewing flowers on tables, of which there are few extant images even though the practice was still current. The aristocracy, particularly in England, had nevertheless begun to replace real petals with flower-embroidered cloths. *Above:* A scattering of wild campanula.

The Rage
for Bouquets

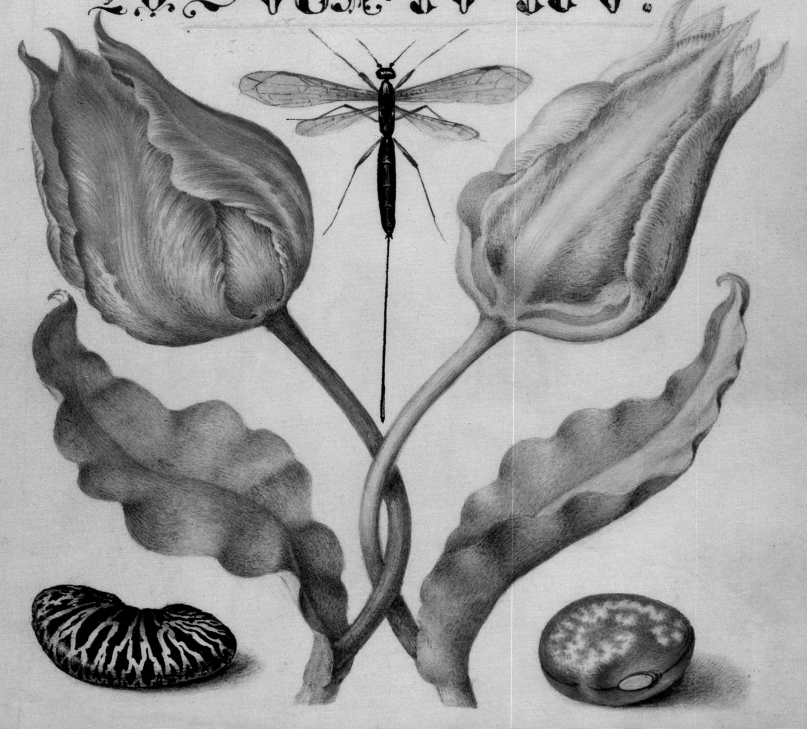

During the seventeenth century, bouquets evolved from a simple bunch of flowers into a precious ornament deploying costly, exotic blooms. Tulips in particular were the focus of a passion and desire for floral rarities. Discovered in a garden in Augsburg in 1559 by Conrad Gesner, they had probably been brought there by Ogier Ghislain de Busbecq (1522–92), ambassador to Constantinople for German Emperor Ferdinand I.

Busbecq's mission was a tricky one, since the empire was under constant threat of Turkish attack. Constantinople was a veritable flashpoint, yet it was also an outstanding nursery for flowers that were almost completely unknown to northern Europe. Busbecq, credited with bringing back several Levantine plants such as lilac and mock orange, was particularly struck by tulips. They already held some mysterious power over Turks. On a certain night in spring, when the moon was full, the entire court would gather at the sultan's palace to admire a floral display of singular beauty—hundreds of vases full of magnificent bouquets of tulips were arranged on platforms, alternating with large crystal balls filled with liquid of various colors. The tulip buds were tightly closed, being sharp and pointed like daggers. Oriental taste would soon be modified by Westerners, however, who tended to prefer their tulips full and round, like a handsome goose egg.

Watercolors by Georg Hoefnagel (1542–1600) (*left*) were among the earliest Western depictions of tulips. This delightful and somewhat magical double illustration shows rainbow colors and curly leaves. The strangeness of these exotic flowers stimulated the imagination, broadening the range of *Garden Delights* as represented in a painting (*above*) by a follower of Frans Vranck (late 16th century). Embroiderers, too, used flowers to extend their repertoire—it was for them that in 1608 Pierre Vallet, master-embroider to French king Henry IV, published an anthology of floral patterns featuring the new bulb plants, his anthology being known as a "florilegium." Whether painted, grown, or embroidered, all these recently imported flowers contributed to the rise in popularity of bouquets. *Previous pages: Bouquet of Flowers* by Rachel Ruysch, c. 1700 (*left*) and *Self-Portrait with Flowers* by Mario dei Fiori, a famous Italian flower painter.

TULIPOMANIA:
A VERITABLE PASSION

Busbecq certainly never imagined the passions that tulips would unleash in Europe when he first wrote to his friend, botanist Carolus Clusius (or Charles de l'Ecluse, 1526–1609), announcing the existence of this pretty flower. The intrigued botanist immediately asked Busbecq to send some bulbs and seeds to Vienna, where Clusius was posted. His true botanical study began only in 1593, after he was named head of the botanical gardens in Leyden, Holland. That was where Clusius systemically cultivated tulips until his death. He experimented with cloning bulbs and noted tulips' strange capacity to metamorphose, suddenly taking on strange colors and curled or fringed shapes. It was not until the nineteenth century that people realized that those fickle beauties—called "broken," "flamed," or "bizarre"—were in fact diseased. A plant virus transmitted by aphids

disturbed a flower's internal functioning and triggered the surprising transformations. Whatever the case, Clusius's experiments determined Holland's horticultural fate. And Leyden became a focal point for scholars and collectors all across Europe, who constantly exchanged bulbs and information with Clusius.

In a matter of years, the tulip's reputation spread like wildfire. A popular new type of anthology, called a "florilegium," presented wonderful portraits of exotic flowers, which inevitably included several "bizarre" tulips among the hyacinths, crown imperials, and multicolored anemones (all originally from Turkey). Such albums were generally catalogues commissioned by rich connoisseurs who wanted to immortalize the precious blooms that spring brought to their gardens. "Garden," however, might not be the right word for their plain flat beds planted with single bulbs at regular intervals; no decorative effect was sought, since owners were more concerned to display their collection of rare and costly species. They were not about to hide them among dense shrubs.

In the seventeenth century, then, gardens of exotic flowers were more like outdoor museums. They were an extension of the "cabinets" where royalty, aristocrats, and bankers proudly displayed every "curiosity" of nature they could find: a bear's jawbone, a branch of coral, the shell of a tortoise. However priceless and unique, such specimens remained inanimate objects. How much more exciting to begin collecting flowers, especially bulbs that returned to life every year! And since the resurrection of tulips, in particular, was often accompanied by fanciful transformations, it is easy to see how they became a prime curiosity.

Meanwhile, burghers all across Europe had become obsessed with imitating the aristocracy. They did not have to be very learned to purchase a few onion-like tulip bulbs, which were already selling at inflated prices. It was the Dutch who proved the most foolish—"tulipomania" raged in

The fine tulips worn in the hair of this *Lady of the Grenville Family with Her Son* (*above*, detail), painted by Gilbert Jackson in 1640, not only add to her charms but also indicate her affluence. This young English lady probably had a wealthy husband whose "cabinet of curiosities" included rare bulb plants and *objets d'art*. *Left:* A detail from *Archdukes Albert and Isabella in a Collector's Cabinet* demonstrates the interest that cultivated men took in flowers. The windows of this study perhaps overlooked a garden, although probably not as profuse the one depicted by Jan Bruegel the Younger when showing *Flora in a Flowering Garden* (*previous pages*). The painting includes fashionable varieties of the day, notably the large crown imperial, imported from the Orient, clearly shown on the right side of the painting with its ring of down-turned flowers reigning over the tulips.

Holland during the 1630s, as demand continued to grow and prices skyrocketed. The commercial value of a tulip depended entirely on aesthetic criteria. The shape of the bloom was important; the seventeenth century liked full and, if possible, double corollas. What counted above all, however, was color—a sphere in which tulips were king. A hierarchy of more or less rare colors was elaborated into a scale of beauty. At the bottom of the ladder were single-color tulips which, while not cheap, were at least affordable. Then came tulips flamed red or violet against a yellow ground. And if such combinations occurred against a white petal, prices reached the stratosphere. The famous "Viceroy"—white bedecked with purple—was worth a fortune, yet still not as much as the red-and-white "Semper Augustus." At the height of tulipomania, the price of one bulb was exceptionally evaluated at 13,000 guilders, that is to say twice the cost of a fine townhouse in a city like Delft.

Tulipomania was a dream shared by dealers and buyers over a pitcher of wine in an inn, where conversation could remake the world. What was really being bought and sold in these watering spots was the hope of making a fortune. The United Provinces of the Netherlands had enjoyed unprecedented prosperity since the founding of the Dutch East India Company in 1602. Everyone wanted a piece of the action—it was not just the rich who got burned in floral speculation. Buying an ordinary bulb that miraculously "flamed" the next spring meant suddenly escaping a past as weaver or carpenter and rising to the silvery mists of Amsterdam's fine canals. It was a big gamble, however, especially when people

Hendrik Gerritszoon's *Floras Mallewagen* (*right*) was painted in 1637, the very year the Dutch tulip market crashed. As an ill wind pushes the wagon toward the sea, Flora sits enthroned with armfuls of tulips, above a group of elegantly dressed but "madcapped" gentlemen drunk on wine. By the end of the seventeenth century, tulips had once again become a simple decorative flower, set in lavish tulip vases specially crafted in Delft porcelain (*above*).

began selling bulbs that were still dormant in the ground. Bills of exchange, instead of the bulbs themselves, were then traded—often on credit, since many speculators had no capital. They waged everything on the assumption that as the season advanced prices would climb still higher, so that the bill could be sold to another purchaser (often no more affluent than the first). And since, to simplify things, negotiations often took place over several glasses of alcohol, people raced headlong into ruin in a mental fog approaching stupor.

By early 1637, Holland was awash with paper millionaires. People started to become suspicious. A rumor made the rounds of Haarlem on 1 and 2 February: sell as soon as possible. By 3 February, it was already too late. Prices collapsed, and many people lost all they had. Needless to say, affection for tulips cooled. Prices dropped considerably throughout the second third of the seventeenth century, although tulips—like all other exotic flowers—remained too expensive and too rare to be found in everyday household bouquets.

DUTCH ARTISTS' ILLUSORY BOUQUETS

The first flower paintings, they say, were made in Antwerp for a lady who asked Jan Bruegel I (called "Velvet Bruegel," 1568–1625) to paint some tulips she could not afford. The painting itself would have been expensive. Artists as reputable as Jan Bruegel worked for a demanding and stickling clientele, and they costed their work by the blossom, indeed by the petal. Tiny details counted—the slightest slip of the brush when painting fine streaks on a tulip or carnation would totally devalue the depicted flower (and largely devalue the painting). Given such hazards and subtleties, painters charged accordingly. The story does not reveal whether the Antwerp lady got her money's worth. The fact is, however, that even before Velvet Bruegel was born, bouquets of flowers had already become the primary subject of several paintings devoid not only of figures but also of any interior setting. The oldest surviving example, signed Hans Memling, is dated 1490. This work was not entirely autonomous, however, since it was painted on the reverse side of a portrait. The new artistic genre was just at its beginnings—only in the seventeenth century would it finally conquer elegant homes where tasteful paintings were hung.

Floral artwork was more than mere fashion—the open conflict raging in Europe between Reformation and Counter-Reformation provided much deeper roots for these painted flowers. Countless blossoms adorned churches in the Catholic city of Antwerp. The clergy was the primary patron of numerous artists who decorated altar paintings and other religious images with garlands of flowers. Magnificent festoons framed images of the Virgin, taunting Protestants who rejected Marian worship and its imagery. This decorative idiom thereby became an Antwerp specialty, cultivating the first generation of flower painters. Apparently, artists of all faiths initially participated, but when persecution began Protestant artists were obliged to flee northward to Holland. Whereas the very Catholic Bruegel remained in Antwerp to the end of his life, Ambrosius Bosschaert the Elder (1573–1645) and Roelandt Savery (1576–1639) left the city, as did dozens of other painters. Their main concern was to build a new clientele. There was no point in seeking patronage from churches (Protestant iconoclasm in the north having eliminated all decoration, even floral), so artists turned to prosperous merchants who appreciated luxury items and were open to innovation. This newly affluent middle class remained in touch with everyday reality and was sensitive to anything that evoked its lifestyle. Thanks to this clientele, the painterly genre known as "still life" evolved in Holland, featuring everyday objects such as tables laden with food and, of course, armfuls of flowers. As anthropologist Jack Goody rightly noted, "the Catholic *couronne* [garland] gave way to the

Hans Memling's *Jug of Flowers* (*above*), painted around 1490 on the reverse side of *Portrait of a Praying Man*, is considered to be one of the first flower pieces. The bouquet still has a devotional significance—the lilies, irises, and columbine symbolize the Virgin's purity and the Passion of Christ (whose monogram can be seen on the vase). Secular flowers began to appear on canvas only in the next century, becoming dominant in the seventeenth century. Flowers were henceforth a part of daily life, and decorated furniture such as this fine tulip cabinet (*left*), painted and inlaid with mother-of-pearl. Its many drawers may have contained flower bulbs.

Protestant, or rather secular, bouquet." Such bouquets would, in fact, soon be blossoming all over Europe.

Flower pieces painted in the first half of the seventeenth century all share the same characteristics, although they obviously betray the personality of individual artists. Paintings by Bosschaert radiate gaily with fresh, luminous blossoms, as though painted on porcelain or enamel. In Savery's work, meanwhile, mysterious chiaroscuro effects and the addition of a few wilting flowers suggest a more melancholy temperament. All artists nevertheless had one thing in common: they never actually saw the bouquets they painted, because such bouquets never existed. Their floral compositions represent a series of implausible arrangements, possible only through artifice. Unrealistic lighting effects underscore the costliest flowers. Every bloom stands out from the rest without ever hiding (or being hidden) by another. Daisies emerge from the top of tall bouquets on impossibly long stems. Furthermore, complete disregard for the seasons allowed artists to place summer roses alongside springtime flowers such as tulips, fritilleries, and irises. Small vases, meanwhile, often contain such a quantity of flowers that they would surely have tipped over—one canvas by Velvet Bruegel includes over 100 varieties alone.

Such bouquets pose a challenge that contemporary florists have tried to meet: in 1995, Dutch florist Marcel Wolterinck reproduced the compositions of Dutch masters for the opening of the Vermeer exhibition at the National Gallery of Art in Washington. He ordered over five thousand flowers in order to be sure the right varieties would be at just the right stage at just the right moment.

The beautiful and crucial *Iris germanica* proved a nightmare, since it flowers only from May to October, and the exhibition opened in November. Wolterinck nevertheless found a grower who supplied a hundred irises—of which only ten blossomed on schedule.

Dutch painters, of course, encountered no such difficulty. Every flower had been studied and sketched in botanical gardens or at collectors' homes. Artists therefore had an abundant floral repertoire at their disposal, regardless of season, for composing their illusory bouquets. Whether the bouquets actually existed or not was irrelevant as long as every flower was botanically correct down to the tiniest detail.

The perfection of such flowers, once hung on a wall in a sitting room, paid constant tribute to the taste and discernment of the lucky owners, some of whom also viewed these paintings as fine objects of meditation.

Bouquets by Ambrosius Bosschaert the Elder, such as this *Vase of Flowers* (*above*, now in the Louvre), were once highly popular. Their bright gaiety was nevertheless contradicted by certain details—here the rose leaves have been attacked by insects, an unpleasant example of which can been seen near the signature. Meanwhile, "Velvet" Bruegel's *Small Bouquet of Flowers* (*right*, now in Vienna), is an entire horticultural show unto itself, displaying flowers from all seasons. Such anachronism is not the only strange feature: at the top, to the left of the large blue iris, a cornflower rises on an impossibly long stem. Note, on the lower right, an unusual but perfectly real flower standing out against the black ground—it is a pretty speckled fritillery, imported from the Orient, whose petals are literally checkered.

THE SYMBOLISM OF FLOWERS

The medieval idea that God had created a world full of countless edifying messages was still current in the seventeenth century, and the search for these hidden meanings became another passion. People who lacked inspiration could always turn to a "book of emblems," or dictionary of elegant epigrams explaining the symbolism of every kind of object, notably flowers. The epigrams were written in such a vague and contorted way that a seeker with any imagination would always find just what was sought. Deciphering nature's own book thereby became a creative game played passionately, indeed obsessively, by pious and/or clever minds.

Fine seventeenth-century flower pieces cannot be understood without this symbolism, which probably added greatly to their popularity. The significance most commonly attached to flowers related to the fragility of their existence, seen as a simile for the transience of human life. This popular theme evolved into the "vanitas" genre, in which fresh flowers bloomed in the sinister presence of a skull, hourglass, watch, or half-eaten ear of corn.

The passing of time was further underscored by the presence of more or less appealing insects—a fly feeding on carrion, a mayfly that lives for only a moment, or a butterfly (whose metamorphosis alludes to resurrection, bringing the sole ray of hope to these works).

Each flower could be individually expressive, even conveying multiple meanings. Roses, for instance, were interpreted in various ways. Ever since antiquity they incarnated the transience of earthly pleasures, the fickleness of love and beauty, and the pangs of desire. Yet that did not prevent the rose from becoming a Catholic symbol of the Virgin or a Protestant emblem of the bloody suffering of Christ and other martyrs (owing to its thorns and redness).

*I*nterpreting the symbolism of flower paintings is a highly complex matter. Dutch artist Anthony van Dyck's 1633 *Self-Portrait with Sunflower* (*above*), has sparked various commentaries. Van Dyck had just moved to England, where he was showered with honors by King Charles I. Since the sunflower was often taken as a symbol of the relationship between king and subjects, Van Dyck could be expressing his loyalty to his monarch. In Dutch literature, however, sunflowers also represented the art of painting, which means that Van Dyck was also vaunting himself! The seventeenth century appreciated ambiguity, as witnessed by its taste for illusionistic effects (*right*), exemplified by this detail from *Trompe l'œil Still Life* by Adrian van der Spelt and Frans van Mieris (1658).

The cult of Flora, goddess of flowers and gardens, underwent a fashionable revival in the sixteenth and seventeenth centuries. People sought ancient, glamorous roots for the new floral cult, overlooking the fact that antiquity viewed Flora as a minor goddess of questionable repute (her celebrations were accompanied by debauchery during which courtesans stripped in public). Thus in 1627, Flora was portrayed as an elegant young lady in *Offering to Flora* (*left*) by the Spanish painter Juan van der Hamen y Leon. The floral realm was also promoted by pretty aristocratic ladies depicted as shepherdesses (*above*)—*Clare Alewijn*, painted by Dirck Santvoort, has decorated her crook with a pair of tulips and a clutch of blossoms bound with gold thread.

Not all flowers had so much to say, however. Nor was that the sole reason for their presence in a bouquet. In fact, many varieties came and went as fashion changed. Crown imperials, whose inverted blooms suggested humility, were adored early in the seventeenth century but became rarer after 1650. The same thing occurred with tulips, which proliferated in the 1630s only to stagnate later. Emblem books did not dwell on tulips, except as an illustration of foolishness, yet the flower earned a certain fame as one of those solar species that open in the morning, follow the course of the sun, and immediately close when the sun sets. Other solar species included marigolds, heliotrope, and above all sunflowers which, although only recently imported from the New World, were immediately associated with royal authority due to a corolla that radiated in every direction. Other new flowers were also charged with meaning. The passion flower, discovered in South America in the sixteenth century, was immediately adopted by the Jesuits (and therefore generally shunned by Protestants), who perceived its unusual arrangement of pistil and stamens as a reminder of the harsh instruments of the crucifixion.

Finally, there was a large repertoire of flowers whose meanings remained unchanged from the Middle Ages. Catholics saw white lilies as an attribute of virginity, whereas violets fluctuated between modesty and frivolity since they were also used to enhance the beauty of dark-haired women. Carnations continued to signify piety, as suggested by their scholarly name, *Dianthus*, which means "flower of God"; long tradition had extended this symbolism to include the holy ties of matrimony, which is why carnations figure in many portraits, both male and female.

Love—conjugal or not—is certainly best expressed with flowers, regardless of time or place. In the seventeenth century, disappointed lovers and shy suitors could always use the language of flowers to express their ardor. The duc de Montausier vainly courted the charming Julie d'Angennes, daughter of the marquise de Rambouillet, for ten long years. He played his last card in 1641 by presenting her with a fine manuscript bound in red leather with a "sweetly fragrant wrapper." Titled *La Guirlande de Julie*, this famous collection of madrigals was illustrated by magnificent paintings of emblematic flowers, every one of which extolled the indifferent lady. Won over, Julie married the duke.

When Julie inherited the Rambouillet residence from her mother, Montausier enthusiastically replanted the gardens. The marquise de Rambouillet's renovation of the chateau in 1620 had revolved entirely around its relationship to the gardens, which could be admired from huge windows in rooms where bouquets were always to be found. The marquise's refined decoration of her salons and bedrooms surprised high society, marking a watershed in the history of interior design. For the first time, a truly harmonious

Medieval floral symbolism continued to be employed at a late date, at least in religious imagery. *Saint Dorothy of Cappadocia* (*above*), by Cesare Dandini (1595–1658), points to roses reddened by the blood of her martyrdom; these simple garden roses also allude to the fact that Dorothy is the traditional patron saint of gardeners. The white lily (*right*), of course, remained the favorite emblem of the Virgin's purity, as illustrated in *The Angelic Greeting* by Eustache Lesueur (1616–55).

approach governed the choice of fabrics as well as the arrangement of furniture, including small tables, inlaid cabinets, and pedestal tables on which flowers could conveniently be displayed. The marquise clearly had a weakness for flowers. Madeleine de Scudéry, who frequented her salon, clearly referred to them in her novel, *Grand Cyrus*: "The air of the palace is always scented—various magnificent baskets full of flowers transform the bedroom into a continual springtime."

The inventory of the marquise's property confirms this impression, for it contains an impressive numbers of vases, certainly including blue-and-white porcelain imported from Ming China. The West had already realized that a fine bouquet called for a fine recipient.

Strangely enough, however, the vases in most paintings remained empty. Almost no paintings depict indoor bouquets—not "real" bouquets, at any rate. There were always beautiful arrangements for special occasions, of course, when an honorable family posed for the artist (as would be done today for a photograph). Too many symbols lurk in those flowers, however, which makes them suspect. Nor are there many portraits in which a woman is shown arranging a bouquet; in the few that exist, the sitter is clearly pointing to the flower that best reflects her condition or mood. The inference is that bouquets had not yet become an everyday affair, especially since the aristocracy liked only splendid, fancy, exotic flowers—hard to have every day!

Yet even if bouquets of fresh flowers were only slowly entering everyday interiors, they already had some loyal fans.

With the emergence of early concepts of interior decoration in the seventeenth century, the aristocracy discovered the comfort and delights of remaining at home. Bouquets of flowers thereby became an everyday feature of domestic life, slowly losing their scholarly and symbolic connotations. The vase of flowers in an engraving (*above*) by Wenzel Hollar (1607–77) probably has general, rather than specific, significance: winter has just ended, the lady is placing her furs in a chest, and admires spring flowers plucked from her own garden. Equally charming and frivolous is a small glove (*top*), dating from 1630, all embroidered in flowers. Some contemporaries, for that matter, criticized the mania for always interpreting flowers symbolically—except, of course, when they spoke of love, as in the frontispiece to *La Guirlande de Julie* (*right*), a magnificent collection of madrigals illustrated by Nicolas Robert.

An Early Lesson in Floral Artistry

Giovanni Battista Ferrari, a Jesuit priest and eminent professor of Hebrew in Rome, was a flower fanatic. He composed admirable bouquets just for the fun of it. Nor was he alone, since his astonishing 1633 book (*Flora, Seu de Florum Cultura: Libri IV*) mentions many Italian aristocrats who shared his passion.

Slow transportation and long distances from one end of the Italian peninsula to the other did not prevent these connoisseurs from communicating and even dispatching some of their floral bouquets. Flowers traveled on horseback in ingenious, tightly sealed wooden boxes humidified with citrus leaves, and apparently arrived at their destination in perfect condition. Everyone's floral ideas and inventiveness could thus be shared, enabling Ferrari to

Once bouquets became popular, vases made their appearance. "Flower vases," designed exclusively for bouquets, were still a recent invention in the seventeenth century. In Canton, Ming dynasty potters expressly crafted blue and white porcelain vases for Westerners. Also appreciated were crystal vases, whose transparence allowed the stems to be admired, as wonderfully depicted (*above*) in a 1627 *Still Life with Artichokes* by Juan van der Hamen y Leon. *Top:* Much more elaborate vases were conceived in a 1633 book by an Italian author named Ferrari, who described metalwork recipients pierced with little holes—like an incense holder—and containing funnel-shaped water cups inside.

Wreaths became very outmoded once bouquets came to the fore, except in some religious imagery. Charles La Fosse's *Annunciation* (*top*), painted circa 1685, is ringed by a magnificent festoon of flowers. Another exception concerned allegorical images of ladies as the goddess Flora (*above*). This anonymous *Portrait of a Woman as Flora*, dating from the first half of the seventeenth century, is rather moving: the woman's beauty is reflected in the mirror, while the empty seat opposite her has been heaped with flowers—the wedding carnation in the lady's hand suggests that the person she misses is her husband.

acquire enough knowledge to fill a book and become a veritable master of floral artistry.

The choice and arrangement of flowers advocated by Ferrari reflect the spirit of painted bouquets in their abundance of species and color. A concern for hierarchy also decreed that the lower part of the arrangement comprise masses of full, less remarkable flowers while the most precious subjects figure at the top. Shaped as a tube or pyramid, these bouquets were probably rather stiff, since no greenery was added to soften them. They were not necessarily designed to decorate an interior—the stems are sometimes nicely covered by narcissus leaves, suggesting that perhaps they were to be held in the hand. Ferrari, for that matter, advises giving the completed bouquet a long drink once it has been bound with linen thread, implying that it was not subsequently placed in water. He does not say, on the other hand, how to maintain the freshness of basket arrangements, which he calls "the prettiest in the world." The wicker bottom, for instance, might be strewn with myrtle leaves on which a vertical mat of tulips stands. In order to obtain the required stiffness, a tiny rod of wood or steel is stuck into each stem. This system of "mounted" flowers, which tended to favor firmness over gracefulness, was extensively used in the nineteenth century.

Ferrari and his contemporaries clearly brought an architectural rigor to their compositions. Flowers were worked like an artistic medium, and had to conform to aesthetic conventions. Sometimes their colors were even modified. The floral palette, although exceptionally rich, suffers from a few absences: there is no black, little green, and a surprising lack of blue. But Ferrari had a solution for blue. First he pulverized cornflowers, "which give sky blue," then blended this powder with a "good mixture" of sheep dung soaked in vinegar. A little salt was added, then the mixture combined with soil. A bulb or root planted in this soil would produce blue flowers. Ferrari provided similar recipes and concoctions for altering fragrances, sometimes completely. He even asserted that, with a little care, garlic can be made to smell like a rose!

This taste for floral artifice did not die with the seventeenth century. Yet little by little, delight in botanical precision and a rigid display of costly specimens gave way to a preference for more natural prettiness.

A new generation of Dutch painters, from Jan Davidsz de Heem (1606–83) to Jan van Huysum (1682–1749), heralded the next century's bouquets, composed of windtousled petals and riotous, tumbling blossoms, plus tendrils, twigs, grasses, and masses of leaves—weed-like things, in short, of no material value.

Strangely, still lifes by Dutch painters never include the tulip vases made in Delft, like this extravagant pyramid with a unique compartment for each tulip (*above*). These items appeared only at the end of the seventeenth century, at a time when artists already preferred to depict denser arrangements, such as this *Vase of Flowers* (*right*) painted around 1660 by Jan Davidsz de Heem. The Delft tulip vases would have yielded arrangements that seemed too stiff. *Previous pages*: Bartholomeus van Bassen's *Interior with Five Women* is an extremely rare composition; the scene must be set in summer, since a bouquet is placed in the unlit hearth. One of the women is bringing flowers from the garden, while the others are composing arrangements with the tools and thread on the table.

FLORA IN FASHION: FROM FLOWERET TO ORCHIDS

Like Dutch artists, French painters began cultivating artificially wind-blown bouquets that cascaded in a graceful—and highly studied—jumble. The early eighteenth century could not yet envisage the small, spontaneous, charming vases that artists such as Jean Siméon Chardin (1699–1779) would depict fifty years later; flower pieces were still being executed in the magnificent, crystalline style used to glorify Louis XIV. A past master of this style was Jean-Baptiste Monnoyer (1634–99) who, as "flower painter to the king," produced dense compositions in which blooms streamed from—as opposed to being contained within—huge metal basins. Marble balusters, richly ornamented velvet fabrics, and other precious props added to the pomposity of his floral arrangements. As Louis XIV's reign drew to a close, nature was still expected to serve art and culture. The French liked rare flowers that blossomed—at great expense—in greenhouses at Versailles, which also boasted fine orange trees and other frost-sensitive species. Royal gardener André Le Nôtre oversaw the management of these precious nurseries, for Louis XIV wanted royal gardens and celebrations to flower "even in winter." The king's taste in flowers included a strong penchant for tuberoses, which therefore became all the rage in Versailles. Like many gentlemen of his generation, however, he remained above all a collector of rare specimens. The extraordinary

wealth of royal collections was lavishly displayed when baskets and strictly ordered flowerbeds bloomed with out-of-season flowers.

Toward the end of Louis XIV's reign, however, the aristocracy wearied of conventional pomp that left so little room for emotion and reverie. In order to escape the rigors of court ceremonial, aristocrats delighted in country outings and open-air pleasures, thereby inventing a new activity that eventually became enormously popular in high society—botanical excursions. Starting in 1690, eminent professors at the Royal Gardens (officially established in Paris in 1640) organized rural outings open to all. Everyone came, from apprentice apothecaries to scholarly collectors to visiting foreigners and, ultimately, socialites. Nothing was more fun than heading out of town to observe "how plants grow naturally." Women willingly joined these outings, especially after 1735 when Swedish naturalist Carolus Linnaeus, who confirmed the existence of sexual reproduction among flowering plants, published a new system of botanical classification so wonderfully simple that "even women could aspire to learn it." Jean-Jacques Rousseau, who made many botanical excursions toward the end of his life, expressly compiled "darling little herbals . . . at once charming and precious" for his female friends. These tiny anthologies, reputedly handier and more practical, were so pretty as to suggest that the infatuation with botany was largely frivolous.

Love of flowers in the second half of the eighteenth century was certainly lively and authentic,

At the dawn of the eighteenth century, a great wave of change came over bouquets, as can be seen (*left*) in Jan van Huysum's *Bouquet of Flowers* (1710). The red-and-gray tulip at the top of the arrangement is turned away from the viewer, which would have been unthinkable earlier. Furthermore, the large hollyhock leaves, shown upside down, are given great prominence. The importance of foliage underscores the new curiosity for everything that grew and proliferated in fields and gardens. This new interest was also reflected in the vogue for small, decorated herbals—a plate from a herbal (*above*) compiled by Swiss botanist Albrecht von Haller (1708–77) features a dried flower from North America.

but it was above all chic. People flaunted their floral knowledge and rural sophistication in the same way as they wore the latest frippery. They also became infatuated with a given flower as soon as scientific or social novelty brought it to the fore. Even dreadfully plain potato flowers had their moment of glory—they were seen on every breast and jacket once Antoine Parmentier obtained Louis XVI's support in promoting the new root vegetable. This did show, however, that people could henceforth appreciate simple flowers and find them graceful. The earlier hierarchy of costly versus inexpensive blooms no longer held. Charm was what counted, to the great benefit of bouquets. During this same period, bouquets also greatly profited from the arrival of exotic species from every continent. There was plenty to nourish the eighteenth century's insatiable appetite for novelty; as historian Keith Thomas rightly pointed out in *Man and the Natural World* (1983), nothing gave a better sense of change than this constant influx of new flowers.

Europe thereby discovered camellias from China, nasturtiums from Peru, and orchids from South America (which were of course immediately snapped up, becoming a collector's item by the end of the century). The first flowers from "Black Africa," where people had barely ventured, also began to appear. They arrived in France in the 1750s following the botanical expeditions of Michel Adanson, who returned with giant hibiscus flowers, convolvulus, pretty-by-night, petunias, and zinnias. Colorful zinnias were certainly appreciated because they were depicted in small compositions as of 1772. Yet not all exotic flowers were immediately put to decorative use. Camellias, already growing in England, and hydrangea, already present in trial gardens, would not truly be in vogue until the next century. It was all a question of sensibility. Time was also required to acclimatize and improve new species—florists worked constantly at making them still more beautiful. The term "florist," it should be noted, entered English in the early seventeenth century to refer to someone who cultivated or bred new varieties; it was not until the late nineteenth century that it came to mean, as it does today, someone who deals in cut flowers.

The gardens and nurseries of amateur experts, meanwhile, were another source of new and sometimes extraordinary developments. Scientific hybrids and color manipulation constantly enriched the floral repertoire. Certain varieties underwent permanent metamorphosis, as was the case with auricula, a sophisticated primrose also called "bear's-ear." The flowers of this "sweetly scented" variety naturally formed a small round bouquet, making it welcome in both vases and paintings. After various manipulations, the auricula suddenly emerged around 1750 as a bright green flower with a pretty white "eye" tattooed in its center. Then it appeared in all kinds of improbable colors such as slate blue, chamois, cinnamon, and gray-green. Fame obviously

New flowers continued to flood in from every continent. By the late eighteenth century, almost all the varieties found in today's bouquets had been classified. The herbal compiled by the Museum of Natural History in Paris—the most extensive in the world—contains moving testimony to those discoveries. Vigilant care by botanists managed to preserve fine blooms in a state of eternal youth, with a touch of original color. *Above:* An Oriental poppy, dated 1741, from Haller's herbal. *Right:* The very first example of hydrangea, picked by Philibert Commerson in April or May 1771 on what is now Isle de la Réunion, off Africa.

HERB. MUS. PARIS.

followed. Everyone wanted bear's-ears in bouquets and gardens, and collectors took endless trouble over them, pampering them like pets. Some gardeners even claimed they fed the soil raw meat!

The universal frenzy for flowers finally overflowed, invading everything. A patch next to the house was no longer enough—English writer Horace Walpole (1717–97) advocated creating scented bowers for infants' cradles, and suggested bringing greenery into sitting rooms. Flowers began moving indoors. C.C.L Hirschfeld, author of a treatise on gardening published in Leipzig in 1779, even exhorted: "May resting and sleeping places, studies, dining rooms, and baths be swathed in the sweet scent of violet, lily-of-the-valley, rocket, stock, white narcissus, lilies, hyacinth, carnation, and reseda from Egypt!"

This allegory of the *Month of April* by Peeter Snijers (*right*) shows a young lady dressed in garden clothes, telling her servant which flowers to cut. Although dated 1727, the varieties and atmosphere conveyed in this painting still evoke the seventeenth century. A later approach can be seen (*above*) in the *Bouquet in a Sculpted Vase* Jan Frans Eliaerts. Near the neck of the vase is a bunch of brown and white primroses called "bear's-ear"; a midnight blue and white variety can also be seen lower down, among the volubilis.

FANCIFUL FLORAL INTERIORS

Despite Walpole's advice, England—which preached the virtues of naturalness in disheveled gardens—did not launch flower-inspired interiors produced by armies of joiners, cabinet-makers, sculptors, and weavers in the second half of the eighteenth century. Rather, it was in France that small rooms were first painted in fresh colors labeled "mauve," "daffodil," and "peach flower," where woodwork and furniture were carved and inlaid with plant and flower motifs. These enchantments, attributed to the goddess Flora, perfectly expressed the aristocracy's state of mind, epitomized by Antoine Watteau's flirtatious genre paintings known as *fêtes galantes*.

In this bucolic, sentimental atmosphere, Madame de Pompadour (who dubbed herself the "Arcadian shepherdess") promoted the riot of flowers that typified the style associated with the reign of her royal lover, Louis XV. All the resources of the Royal Gardens were mobilized, from lowly gardeners to eminent botanists, whom Madame de Pompadour asked to landscape the grounds around her Versailles "Hermitage"—groves of oleander, pomegranate, and lilacs, arbors of jasmine, and a little corner reserved for scented wild flowers. The Hermitage's ground-level pavilions made it possible to go directly from the gardens into salons decorated in such a floral manner that it became hard to distinguish indoors from out. Everything suggested the delightful budding of an eternal spring, from green-lacquered furniture to Chinese taffeta printed with peonies and birds. The fashion for "chinoiserie," spurred by regular imports of silk and porcelain (which Canton manufactured specially for Westerners), did not aim at authenticity. On the contrary, it stimulated a fanciful approach that probably contributed to the discovery of new floral motifs and artifices.

Madame de Pompadour moreover proposed a new type of floral decoration during a famous reception at Bellevue in November 1750. A contemporary witness described how she received the king and her guests "in an apartment at the back of which was an immense hothouse and bed of flowers, in the midst of a harsh winter. Since fresh roses, carnations, and lilies abounded, the ecstatic King was beside himself with admiration for the beauty and sweet scent of this flowerbed. But nature had been fooled. Everything was of porcelain—vases, roses, carnations, lilies, and stems—and the sweet scent of these divine flowers was the effect of the artful dissipation of their essences." Those exquisitely fine objects were the speciality of a porcelain manufactory in Vincennes. The small factory was already known for its pretty flowers, which could be found nowhere

Madame de Pompadour (*above*) was one of the people behind the rage for flowery decors. She liked to appear wreathed in flowers, as in this 1756 portrait by François Boucher. She is wearing a green court gown trimmed with silk roses, and is surrounded by charming floral motifs—the carved clockcase shows a cherub sleeping among garlands of flowers, the Chinese silk cushions are decorated with peonies, and real roses are set at her feet and on her books. While all kinds of fanciful forms were created throughout the century, people continued to hark back to the floral practices of antiquity (*left*), as illustrated by a detail from *Three Ladies Adorning a Term of Hymen* by Sir Joshua Reynolds (1723–92).

else. Louis XV bought up the entire Vincennes stock and transferred production to Sèvres, triggering the Sèvres manufactory's famous floral period, when it developed the soft red "Pompadour rose" that decorated vases, tea cups, and chocolate services.

The marvels invented at Vincennes were adapted to all kinds of ornament sold by small-wares merchants. One of them, Lazare Duvaux, left a detailed description of them in his order book: baskets of braided wire, lined with silk and filled with a wide variety of porcelain flowers on stems; China or Saxony vases filled in the same way; and "sticks of light," that is to say torches or candelabra composed of "branches imitating nature" on which blossom double anemones, buttercups, campanula, or stock. Duvaux also mentioned another item, purchased by the duc de Francavilla in October 1757: "a dessert centerpiece composed of several Saxony groups and figures, vases of flowers and animals, decorated with gilded and varnished branches, adorned with Vincennes flowers, and placed on a gilded pedestal." Such centerpieces had become the focus of table settings for state dinners, particularly during the dessert course, in the early eighteenth century.

Originally of gold and silver, these fine objects held everything that might be useful during the meal, from salt shakers to oil and vinegar cruets to candles. Yet their functional role was overtaken by more spectacular considerations as center-

pieces became whimsical replicas of palaces, arbors, and gardens. Flowers—both fresh and porcelain—enjoyed pride of place in an escalating competition to surprise and enchant guests. All materials could be used, provided that the results looked convincing. So confectioners, including a certain Travers, concocted an inexpensive new floral element that conformed to the imagination's every whim, namely a sugar paste that could be molded into extravagant garlands, flowerbeds, and bouquets which were then oven-dried and painted with fine brushes.

People swooned in the delightful confusion of all these real and imitation flowers. European courts from Prussia to Russia succumbed to the irresistible charms of Paris fashion. England, ever eclectic, added the French style to its Gothic, neoclassic, and Chinese repertoire. Textile manufacturers in London, Jouy, Lyon, and Berlin churned out yards of decorative fabrics which, by tradition, were more conducive to floral patterns than any other medium. "Fancy" and "whimsical" flowers snaked along silks produced by Jean-Baptiste Pillement (1728–1808), who traversed Europe with his designs. And painter Philippe de La Salle (1723–1804), well-known in France, Austria, Spain, and the court of Russia, decorated his elaborate brocaded fabrics with profuse bouquets.

Similarly, floral prints began their lasting career on calico, a patterned cotton initially imported by the East India Company but hence-

Haberdashers used to sell all kinds of artificial flowers, like the silk ones depicted in Luis Paret's *La Boutique* (*above*, detail). The merchant is opening a small chest of flowers, the woman is admiring a floral diadem, and her friend is discussing prices. Such trinkets were very expensive, if cheaper than the porcelain variety also found at a haberdashery. There are few vestiges today of these highly fragile flowers. Yet thanks to Didier Gardillou, a contemporary French artist who employs the techniques once used in the Vincennes porcelain manufactory, these marvellous blooms exist once more in all their freshness (*right*).

forth manufactured in Europe. Fresh and colorful calico transformed interior decoration, competing with the silk it replaced on summer furnishings. In every season, meanwhile, wallpaper—another eighteenth-century innovation—spread floral motifs everywhere. The English enthusiasm for Chinese papers showing swarms of butterflies gathering nectar from wisteria, chrysanthemums, and irises, contributed to an early infatuation with this new style of "tapestry." Later, around 1770, French manufacturer J.–B. Réveillon spurred the fashion for wallpaper panels decorated in plant-inspired arabesques.

Wallpaper was constantly brought up to date and taste, becoming almost as ephemeral as the bouquets it depicted—from one year to the next, fashionable flowers paraded across it. This catalogue of floral art was fleshed out by an infinite range of compositional devices (flowers beribboned, hung, garlanded, in vases, or in bunches), yielding bold results that are ultimately quite similar to the work of today's florists.

Rather sophisticated designs had a flowering bush emerging from a large cabbage, or combined bouquets with strawberries, redcurrants, and sliced melons. Some combinations, probably reflecting actual use, were even bolder: wide strips of spotted fur—panther or leopard skins— were knotted at regular intervals by clusters of roses.

The way cut flowers were bound, moreover, seemed to be the object of great care. They might be gathered or tied by gold thread, strips of satin and lace, or—the clear favorite—blue ribbon. Ribbon alluded to the feminine world, since women kept a range of it on the vanity table. Ribbons were an indispensable accouterment of stylish dress—as were bouquets.

Eighteenth-century floral wallpaper is highly instructive. It indicates which flowers were fashionable, which arrangements were in vogue, and other intriguing details. On French wallpaper, for example, flower stems were often cut at an angle, yet on English paper they are cut straight. The difference is hard to explain, but specialists occasionally use it to determine the origin of certain patterns. *Top:* A fragment of Prieur-style wallpaper, c. 1780. *Above:* A model for wallpaper with large, feathery carnations from the Jacquemart and Benard firm, 1799. *Right:* Braids of flowers on the chandeliers suggest a shower of petals in this *Banquet at the Redoutensaal*, Vienna, painted in 1760 by a follower of Martin Mytens.

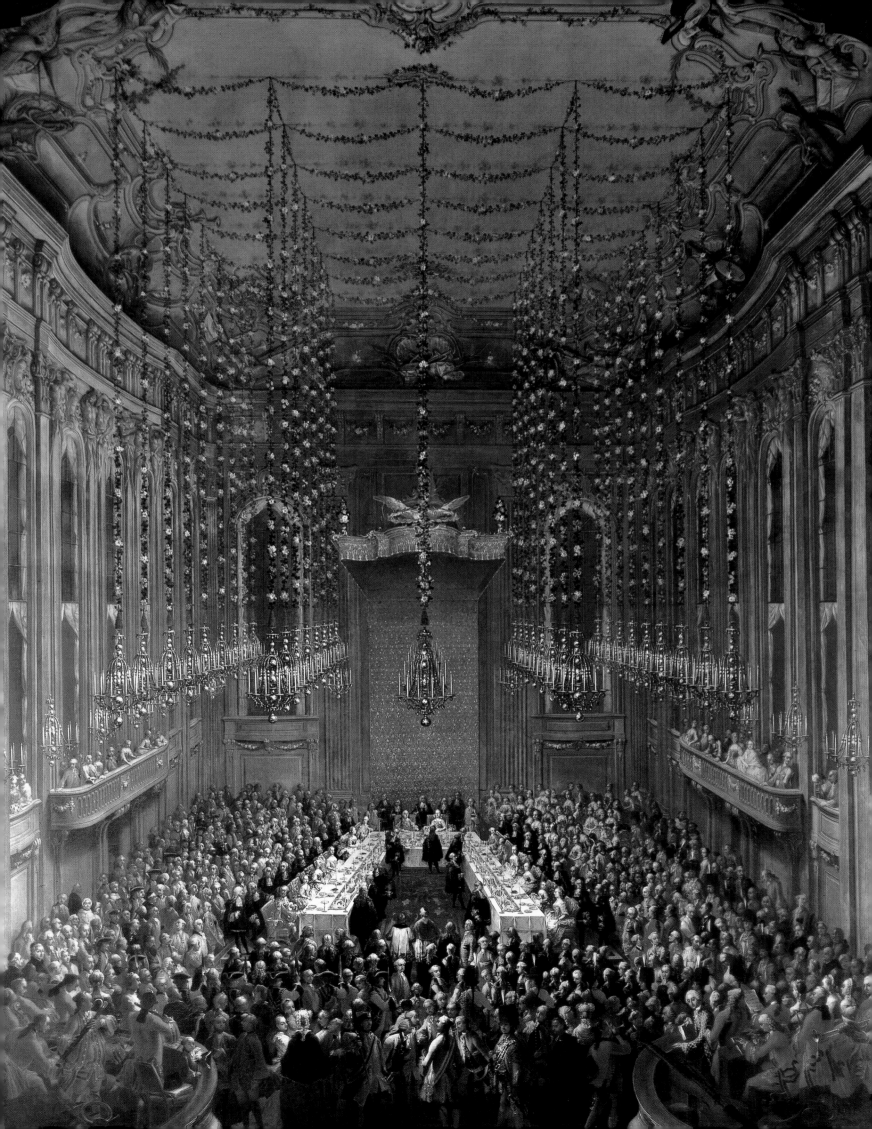

BOUDOIR BOUQUETS

In 1771, P.- J. Buc'hoz, an eclectic author who wrote on subjects as disparate as hot springs, tobacco, and the life of moles (!), published a treatise titled *Toilette de Flora, ou Essai sur les plantes et les fleurs qui peuvent servir d'ornement aux dames* (*Flora's Toilette, or, An Essay on Plants and Flowers Used to Adorn Ladies*). This beauty guide was partly devoted to the concoction of plant-based balms, lotions, and oils designed to whiten teeth, eliminate wrinkles, dye gray hair, and remedy all those other age-old complaints. Of more relevance here, however, is the chapter devoted to the floral decoration of a "vanity," referring to not only the table itself but also the cloth covering it. This piece of furniture was theoretically for private use, yet could be quite costly, as could the cloth scented with spices and floral powders. In fact, the vanity table became the key prop of a highly staged scene once eighteenth-century ladies began receiving visits while at their toilette. A morning rendezvous allowed them to make a show of seductiveness, with their hair down and dressed in a falsely casual gown. Needless to say, the "real" dressing had taken place in private, well before the arrival of admirers or lovers.

The learned Buc'hoz recommends to his readers a range of flowers which, placed on a lady's vanity table, will enhance her charms. His book thereby provides information on everyday bouquets, which were obviously quite different from

the festive or sophisticated compositions immortalized on fabrics and wallpapers. Almost all the flowers Buc'hoz mentions are fairly common and, when in season, easy to find in gardens, country homes, or fields. He lists mullein with its "long stalks of yellow flowers that make a pretty pyramid," columbine, several varieties of honeysuckle, caper plants whose "pretty flower is highly appreciated," apple flowers and double colchicum. Since certain species were not appropriate for a vanity table, Buc'hoz recommends other uses for them. Crown imperial and other fritilleries, campion, stock, and potted impatiens were more suited to the everyday decoration of large interiors.

Yet if Buc'hoz took the trouble to extol their aesthetic qualities in a book aimed at women, that is because indoor flowers, from the boudoir to the sitting room, had clearly become the domain of the mistress of the house. It was a charming preoccupation worthy of the attention of idle gentlewomen. They probably devoted much time to it, since they also had to choose the small floral clusters that went in their hair or on their breast. To this end they made pompons of pomegranate flowers, cornflowers, or cowslips. Flat "trimming bouquets," pinned along the edge of a low neckline, might combine pansies, larkspur, anemones, buttercup and bear's-ear (this latter highly prized because it "lasted").

Obviously, all these floral ornaments had the natural defect of being ephemeral, wilting in the feverish heat of a ball. A few solutions existed, if rather inconvenient. Madame d'Oberkirch, an

Baroness de Neubourg-Cromière (*right*) deploys a full range of fashionable floral devices in this portrait by Alexander Roslin (1718–93)—rose garlands and ruffles on the dress, petals stuck in the hair, and an indispensable corsage, generally worn on the left shoulder. Corsages, or "side bouquets," became fairly substantial from the 1770s, and included brand new blooms such as zinnias and arum lilies, whose whiteness set off fair complexions. *Above:* A rose placed on a *Wine Glass* by Herman van der Mijn (1684–1741).

While at the dressing table in the morning, women would choose the flowers to be worn that day. Many paintings and engravings illustrate this intimate moment when ladies sat in front the mirror trying out corsages or hair ornaments. The scene might even occur en famille, as suggested by a *Group Portrait* painted in 1756 by François-Hubert Drouais (*right*). Note that the gentleman also sports floral patterns on his Chinese dressing gown. Around 1780, dandies would even wear corsages, like women. *Above:* Details of an embroidered garment (*top left*) and (*top right and above left and right*) brocaded fabrics from the eighteenth century (private collections).

Alsatian aristocrat who wrote her memoirs in 1789, documents a method that only added to the discomfort of court dress. Invited to Versailles in 1778, where the Queen "was performing a comedy at Trianon," Madame d'Oberkirch donned court dress and recounted how, for the first time, she tried "something very much in fashion but rather uncomfortable—flat little bottles, curved to the shape of the head, containing a little water for soaking the stems of natural flowers, keeping them fresh in the hair." Fortunately, this discomfort could be avoided by following the shrewd advice of "fashion merchants" such as Mademoiselle Pompée, Madame Eloffe, and the "divine" Rose Bertin, all as famous in their day as haute couture designers are today. These experts in artifice knew how to prettify gowns and hair by adding masses of flowers in the form of garlands and bouquets that were as ravishing as they were fake. Their artificial trimmings were a deceptively good copy of nature, making all kinds of floral extravagance possible. In theory, however, only young women whose complexion could match the sheen of flowers were free to bedeck themselves as they wished. With age, it was thought wiser to abandon this kind of finery—Marie-Antoinette had just turned thirty in 1786 when she declared that she would no longer wear "the color pink, or flowers," since they would appear "ridiculous at [her] age." Yet so many women refused to recognize their own advancing years that the production of artificial flowers hardly suffered from this taboo.

In addition to the artificial bouquets of sugar paste or porcelain already discussed, other materials such as velvet, silk, and parchment were used for floral decorations on clothes or in the home. The garlands of flowers—probably artificial—seen attached to beds and woodwork were comparable in every way to the ones that swirled along skirts. By 1780, it would seem that production of fashion trimmings was sufficiently large to constitute an autonomous sector of the artificial flower industry, which was then booming, particularly around All Saints' Day and Pentecost when gardens were stripped of everything. A flowermen's guild called *bouquetiers* in French had the exclusive right to make these accessories, which were far from novel. China had long produced illusionistic flowers, and Italy had taken up the tradition with such materials as feathers, fabric, and even silk-worm cocoons, which took colors well and imitated the velvety texture of blossoms. Italian products were so realistic, moreover, that the French often referred to the finest floral trimmings as "Italian flowers." Their only drawback was the exorbitant cost—the poorly equipped Italians took an inordinate amount of time to cut each petal and leaflet with scissors. Manufacturing techniques would be perfected in Paris, first by a certain Seguin who successfully entered the imitation flower business in 1738 by inventing crinkling irons, pressing irons, and all kinds of specific tools. Later, a Swiss competitor invented both a punch, making it possible to cut several identical elements at once, and an

The small, simple household bouquet of garden and wild flowers was an eighteenth-century invention. Jean-Baptiste Chardin (1699–1779) was the artist who perhaps best conveyed all its charm, as seen in this *Flower Piece* (*above*). Such spontaneous, natural arrangements reflected the influence of women and their use of flowers, whether real or silk. A 1762 portrait of a Danish lady (*left*) by Peter Cramer shows *Anna Marie Koster* at a table making bouquets of silk flowers with the ribbons and thread seen in her work-basket.

embosser for imprinting fine veins on leaves.

By the end of the eighteenth century, Paris was the leading flower manufacturer. Eleven major workshops existed, including the highly reputed firm of a Bohemian entrepreneur named Wenzel, who made a famous—and disturbingly life-like—rose for Marie-Antoinette, cut entirely from the fine skin of an eggshell. Wenzel taught a few tricks of the trade to court ladies, who enjoyed making that sort of thing. They probably never dreamed how handy these skills would turn out to be, not having dreamed that revolution and exile would oblige some of them to earn a living. So totally unprepared were they for their change in fortunes, that for certain aristocratic ladies the only way—or at any rate the only suitable way—to survive was to make flowers. Madame de Genlis, who in better days had been governess to the children of the Orléans family, had no hesitations about making flowers for a living. Others followed her example, especially once word got around that Christiane Vulpius, Goethe's wife, had herself been working in a Weimar flower factory when she met her genius of a husband. Such anecdotes made the floral craft considerably more respectable!

The fresh-cut flower trade was another story altogether. It, too, was entirely feminine,

but in no way respectable. This was a street affair—harsh, exposed, and practically unstructured since "flower girls" had no shops. The situation became even more precarious when the French Revolution deprived them of former guild privileges; under the monarchy they had enjoyed a certain social status, whereas they henceforth had to compete with "unprofessional and unscrupulous wenches." The resulting arguments and street scuffles required frequent police intervention.

Ultimately, this picturesque disarray reflected the eighteenth-century image of flowers. They had permanently entered the female sphere of influence, invading feelings and fashion as well as interior decoration. Everything remained disorganized, however. Flowers were still itinerant, sold in haphazard fashion. Nor was anything codified. Friends and lovers probably gave flowers to each other, but contemporary manuals of etiquette make absolutely no reference to codes of exchange. How different things would become in the next century, when a well-turned-out florist in the form of a pleasant maiden awaited the arrival of customers in her shop. And those customers would be difficult and demanding, fully conversant in the language of flowers and the strict rules of floral savoir-faire.

The love-letter and little bouquet in Jean Honoré Fragonard's *Billet Doux* (*left*, detail) remain delightfully ambiguous—the writing on the envelope does not make it clear whether she has just received the missive or is about to send it. French novelist Philippe Sollers is highly intrigued by this mystery, as he writes in *Les Surprises de Fragonard*: "It's quite disturbing, I thought the letter was being received, not sent. Unless it's being intercepted. Is she a spy? Who knows? This beautiful red-head, with her beckoning, sidelong glance, must have more than one trick up her sleeve." *Above:* Jean-Baptiste Huet's *Flower Girl.*

Say It

With

Flowers

The confusion following the French Revolution, in which flower girls struggled to survive, was accompanied by a relative loss of interest in flowers. It took time to get over the Ancien Régime's floral excesses which, like all visible signs of wealth, were associated with a corrupt aristocracy. Yet revolutionary citizens ultimately sought to enliven their everyday lives. Since reactionary Catholic rituals had become suspect, dangerous beliefs were channeled into the cult of the goddess Nature, in the form of small temples of foliage and blooms, especially wild flowers picked along the roadside or from the ruined gardens of the fallen monarchy. The chosen flowers had to be "politically correct," which meant avoiding overly showy varieties such as roses, entire fields of which were occasionally uprooted by the republican government in order to plant food crops.

A democratization of floral customs, previously the exclusive domain of an elite, thus dawned. The trend continued to grow throughout the nineteenth century, first manifested by an increase in purchases of potted flowers. In a memoir dated 1811, a certain Pujoulx noted that "in the past twelve or fifteen years, the cultivation of many curious plants, once relegated to botanical gardens, has become a widespread fashion. This fashion passed from rich people to the class of people who have only a modest fortune… On parish feast days, instead of bringing a simple bouquet of flowers that wilts within hours, people bring plants in pots." A twice-weekly market specializing in floral items had already existed in Paris at the end of the eighteenth century. Squeezed on to Quai de la Mégisserie, in a space that normally hosted a scrap metal market, it was soon unable to meet the needs of Parisians. In 1800 it therefore moved to the other bank of the Seine, where the capital's first true flower market was founded on what is still famously known as Quai aux Fleurs. Ten other markets of this type would emerge during the nineteenth century, an initiative copied all across Europe, launching the charming and inexpensive habit of "picking up some flowers at the market." Little city balconies and casement windows began sprouting flowers that would once have been considered true rarities. They were grown in clay pots, chests, baskets, or in the elegant flowerboxes that

In 1789, poppies could be seen everywhere. Their mere presence on a sample of wallpaper (above) from the Réveillon firm is enough to date it. It was entirely coincidental that 1789 was also the year of the French Revolution, but poppies thereby retain a patriotic connotation. In any case, they heralded a democratization of floral habits. Once ladies began dressing in bourgeois fashion, a simple bouquet of wild flowers was all the artifice they needed, as seen in Jacques Louis David's portrait of Madame Pierre Seriziat *(right). By the early nineteenth century, rare species were grown on windowsills where previously such plants had been the preserve of the aristocracy (top)—Martinus Rorbye's* View from the Artist's Window *dates from the 1820s.* Previous pages: The Birthday Cake, *1877, by Franz Verhas (left) and* A Box at the Théâtre des Italiens *by Eva Gonzalèz, c. 1874 (right).*

became an indispensable decorative element of Empire homes.

Architects and decorators Charles Percier and P.F.L. Fontaine, who forged French imperial taste, immediately saw the advantages to be drawn from "flower tables." Generally arranged in pairs in order to respect the sacrosanct rule of symmetry, they lent a touch of sensuality to otherwise austere Empire interiors. They also perfumed the air, especially since such compositions included large clusters of violets, which Napoleon apparently liked. The modest violet thereby acquired political significance, and would be worn on the lapel of convinced bonapartists, only suddenly to disappear from breasts and windowboxes in the early days of the Restoration. Their disappearance was short-lived—on 11 January 1816, Louis XVIII surprised everyone by casually handing around bouquets of violets to speechless ladies, whom he reassured with the words, "Please take them, I've included violets in the amnesty."

After the purgatory of the revolutionary years and the spare elegance of the Empire, flowers made a big return to Restoration France. They were deliberately deployed to celebrate the return of the Bourbons and monarchic values, although extravagance was avoided. The moderate use of flowers in France was a long way from the profusion of plants then transforming chic Russian and Austrian interiors into veritable

Marie-Louise of Austria's Arrival in Compiègne with Napoleon I, as depicted by Pauline Desmarquets Auzou (*above*), was bedecked with flowers. It is worth noting, however, that Marie-Louise, in deference to her imperial husband's taste, chooses a wreath of violets. Napoleon's first wife, Joséphine (*far right*), had preferred roses. The diadem of roses seen in this miniature portrait was made of silk flowers, the invoice for which—drawn up when she was still empress—reveals her fondness for this type of head-dress, so fashionable at the time.

Salon de Fleurs de S. M. l'Impératrice & Reine.

Mad: Roux-Montagnat Rue Helvétina, N°. 16.

Paris, le

Vendu à Sa Majesté l'Impératrice & Reine

avoir remonté une coiffure de roses blanches fondues en couleur de chair et fourni 4 roses idem	24
fourni une coiffure de roses roses	72
1 Coiffure en Agrostidas	72
1 Coiffure en roses épanouies	72
1 Coiffure de fleurs de Champs	72
1 Coiffure de rose roses et Jasm	72
1 Coiffure de Marguerites a cœur puce	72
2 en ½ garnitures de robe en fleurs de	150
1 Coiffure œillets roses	72
1 Diadème de roses et une Guirlande de ¾ idem	96
1 Coiffure en renoncule	96
1 Coiffure en oreille d'ours	72
1 Coiffure belle Bruyère	72
remonté 1 Diadème en fleur Mélangée et fourni des fleurs	24
ton et emballage	9
	1047

arbors, which so fascinated the naturalist Bory de Saint-Vincent on his arrival in Vienna in 1805. "I remember, among others, the intoxicating boudoir of the comtesse de C. You reached it via veritable bushes of African heather, hydrangea, and camellias, then quite rare, planted on flowerbeds further garnished with violets and other flowers growing densely like lawn." Vegetation also invaded German interiors, giving birth to the *Zimmerlaube* or "bedroom arbor," a kind of trellised screen on which ivy and climbing flowers grew. France was not yet ready for such foreign innovations, however.

THE PALAIS-ROYAL: THE FIRST PARISIAN FLOWER SHOP

The taste for flowers initially resurfaced through evocations of the past, of the reassuring permanence of things. Then the continuity of floral customs was best expressed by artists. Many painters who had already been working in the eighteenth century transmitted their skills to the post-revolutionary generation. The career of Pierre-Joseph Redouté (1759–1840) is exemplary in this respect. It began at Versailles, where his talent won him the post of draftsman to Marie-Antoinette. The fact that he became known as the "painter of roses and professor of queens" in no way blocked a later appointment to the Museum of Natural History during all the revolutionary turmoil, in order to continue the former king's famous series of botanical drawings. Redouté subsequently became Empress Joséphine's patented artist, immortalizing the splendors of her Malmaison garden in a series of 120 plates. The artist having become a monarchic fixture, the Bourbon restoration overlooked his bonapartist connections. He published *Roses* in 1817, was

awarded the Légion d'Honneur in 1825, and survived the revolution of 1830 without falling into disgrace. He died suddenly one day in 1840 in the Museum of Natural History, while examining a lily a student had brought him.

Redouté's roses and lilies delighted flower lovers of every stripe. His work remained unaffected by political change—at least in appearance. In fact, Redouté's habits changed somewhat in the 1830s. Until then, he had always picked his models in royal or imperial parks, or took whatever he needed from the Botanical Gardens. Yet suddenly, despite his rank, he suddenly behaved like everyone else, buying his pretty—and sometimes rare—flowers from Madame Prévost, a flower merchant in the arcaded courtyard of the Palais-Royal. No ordinary flower girl, Madame

More than any other painter, Pierre-Joseph Redouté was able to capture the grace and freshness of flowers, as conveyed by this *Vase of Roses (left)*. French novelist Colette was still charmed by his work one hundred years later: "The flower completed, he would place a drop or gem of dew that he used like a killing beauty mark. He was the artist who taught princesses to paint and anemones to weep. Anemones, endless roses, bear's-ear— everything in nature with a velvety bloom melts into tears under Redouté's brush." *Above: Bouquet of Lilies and Roses in a Basket on a Small Chiffonier* by Antoine Berjon (1754–1802).

Prévost was practically a modern "florist," established in a shop so small that three people could barely squeeze in. It was nevertheless a real shop, the first in Paris and perhaps in Europe. This innovation, widely commented upon at the time, was not without significance insofar as it altered floral habits: as opposed to making a small, spontaneous purchase from the basket of a flower girl on the street, Redouté entered into discussions

"composed" bouquets of stemless blooms attached to a reed. Because they could not be watered, such arrangements withered fairly rapidly. These artifices were nevertheless dictated by the fashion for flat and pyramidal bouquets, which Genoa had made a specialty. Stems were of no importance when it came to pressing blossoms against one another to form a kind of mosaic of colors. The natural bunches of flowers sold by Madame

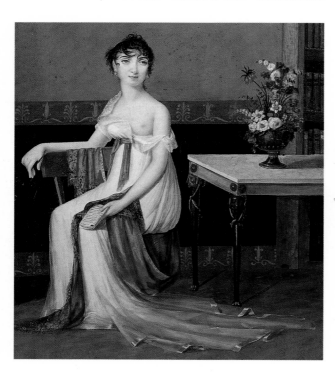

with his florist, took her advice, appreciated her talent and her fine merchandise.

Dozens of boutiques opened in the wake of Madame Prévost. And yet she was not imitated when she launched the fashion for "bouquets that last," by which she meant long-stemmed bunches that would last several days if the water in the vase were replenished. As surprising at this may seem, such bouquets were an incredible novelty. Since the sixteenth century, flower girls had mainly sold

Prévost were nevertheless similar to bouquets people arranged for themselves at home. Pretty compositions on the vanity tables of eighteenth-century ladies were certainly free from artifice. Similarly, the bouquets that Félix composed for Madame de Mortsauf in Balzac's *Lily of the Valley* (1835) had all the grace and suppleness of wild flowers. His spiraling convolvulus, umbellate chervil, and corkscrewing ivy was the antithesis of Genoese bouquets. Félix was making no attempt

Following the relative austerity of the Napoleonic Empire, the Bourbon Restoration revived the Ancien Régime's more lavish floral practices. Although moderation prevailed when it came to interior decoration, clothing became a veritable orgy of flowers. Compare the anonymous portrait of a young woman with bare breast (*above left*), dated 1801, with a 1814 print (*right*) published in the magazine *Le Bon Genre* over the caption, "Flower Mania." Wreaths of fresh flowers, meanwhile, highly appreciated during the imperial period due to their allusion to antiquity, fell out of fashion. *Above right: Garland of Pansies* by Antoine Pascal (1803–59).

Bouquets were henceforth appropriate on all occasions. The family patriarch, surrounded by his family, is offered a whole series of bouquets in Michel Genod's *Wishing Great-Grandfather Happy Returns* (1838). These stiff, crested bouquets were probably composed of blooms lashed to a reed, a common practice at the time.

to create floral architecture, he simply wanted to send the lady he loved a message—which she privately decoded, delighted by what she read. Indeed, flowers became eloquent once again in the nineteenth century. And since they spoke of love, everyone thought the message was simple.

THE LANGUAGE OF FLOWERS

In his article of 1993, "Say It With Flowers," Brent Elliot, librarian at the Royal Horticultural Society, provided an interesting analysis of the famous language of flowers that so preoccupied nineteenth-century society. His article is mischievously subtitled, "Don't Send a Bouquet if You Want to be Clearly Understood," because this incredibly complicated language varies according to author, period, and country. At the risk of disappointing people who would like to believe in a kind of floral esperanto, it should be clearly

stated that floral grammar is nothing more than a pleasant delusion.

Between 1840 and 1880, a multitude of books entitled *The Language of Flowers* were published all across Europe and the United States. These books claimed to derive from various—conflicting—sources. Among French specialists, it was said that the language of flowers was Turkish in origin, and that it had first been imported into England by Lady Mary Wortley Montagu, a friend of Alexander Pope. This double pedigree—oriental and English—was glamorous enough to convince skeptics. Lady Mary indeed alluded to a strange mode of communication in 1718 by sending one of her friends a "Turkish love-letter," which turned out to be a box of various objects, each accompanied by a line of verse indicating its meaning. Although the box indeed contained a jonquil, a rose, and a blade of straw, it also held a piece of soap, a lump of coal, a pea, a clove, a pearl, and some paper. So the message was not strictly floral, and the meaning

"Césarine was dressed in white crêpe, with a wreath of white roses on her head, and a rose at her side; a shawl chastely covered her shoulders and chest—she drove Popinot mad." Balzac's literary portrait in *César Birotteau* is a perfect pendant to Théodore Chasserieu's portrait of *Mademoiselle de Cabarrus* (*left*). These marriageable young ladies were dressed to please yet carefully retained their innocence. The only thing they knew of love—until their wedding day—was the adulterated version suggested by "the language of flowers." *Above:* A very limited selection of the countless books on the language of flowers published between 1840 and 1880.

attributed to each object was above all determined by the poetic effect of a perfect rhyme. In short, the Turkish origin of the language of flowers is unfounded, even if the nineteenth century continued to refer with conviction to oriental bouquets composed like a riddle.

Floral language stems much more surely from a specialization of seventeenth-century symbolism which, as mentioned above, was not limited to flowers. An early attempt was the 1641 *Guirlande de Julie*. Yet it was not until 1819 that a "language of flowers" as we know it today appeared for the first time—in Paris. The author was a certain Charlotte de Latour, an aristocratic pseudonym adopted by Louise Cortambert, wife of geographer Eugène Cortambert. Her book was organized around the months of the year, giving in seasonal order the name of blossoming flowers, their meaning, and historical references or anecdotes relating to them. The end of the book included two charts for practical use: an alphabetical index of flowers (along with a brief summary of their attribute), and a most convenient dictionary of the vast range of moods likely to be conveyed by a bouquet. If you wanted to suggest "ulterior motives," for instance, you should send large-blossomed asters, or jonquils to indicate "desire," or peonies for "shame." Thanks to these alphabetical charts, it became possible to encode—or decode—a bouquet. That was not all, however. The book also contained a floral clock, attributing a specific variety to every hour of the day, plus a letter composed of flower drawings which produced one message if read right-side-up and another one entirely if turned upside-down. Exercises such as this were far from simple and required a great deal of enthusiasm, or a great deal of time. Yet it was precisely this complexity that people liked.

Charlotte de Latour was followed by a number of other French authors. Some of them attempted to give the language of flowers a more botanical, scholarly turn. Others tried to moralize it a little, insofar as the system was of course primarily a method of communication between the two sexes. Many female authors tried to forestall dangerous reveries by providing a list of potential meanings that blithely omitted "sensuality," "burning with desire," "surrender," and "ecstasy, I love you."

Latour's book was translated into German in Berlin in 1820. The first English translation dates from 1827, and became an enormous bestseller, being reprinted nine times in the next twenty years. Other British writers soon moved into the field, and divergences from the meanings employed in the French model immediately appeared. Latour's attributions were initially copied directly, yet were sometimes poorly transcribed from one language to the other, creating new symbolic meanings based on nothing more than a translator's error. Moreover, English culture already had its own floral allusions, often based on Shakespeare. Ophelia's flowers had enjoyed a conventional meaning for over two centuries. It would have been unthinkable, for

Flowers could not only speak, they could also assume bodily form. A flower played a leading role in Taglioni's 1827 ballet, *Le Zéphyr et la Rose*, as well as in Théophile Gautier's famous poem, *Le Spectre de la Rose*, for which Berlioz composed a score in 1841. In the same spirit, the famous illustrator Grandville published his fantasmagorical *Fleurs Animées* in 1847 (*above*), which featured half-human, half-floral creatures like "the Orange Flower Bride." *Right:* An English fan could be used simultaneously as a dance card and a symbolic dictionary of flowers. *Far right:* A popular illustrated "language of flowers" published in Metz, France, around 1850.

LE LANGAGE DES FLEURS.

Amaranthe. (Constance.) — Absinthe. (Peines de cœur.) — Campanules. (Flatterie.) — Digitale. (Travail.)

Dipsacus, Chardon. (J'ai soif.) — Eglantier. (Eloquence.) — Géranium écarlate. (Bêtise.) — Hortensia. (Beauté froide.)

Iris. (Bonne nouvelle.) — Lis. (Majesté, pureté.) — Mauve. (Amour maternel.) — Petite Marguerite ou Paquerette. (Innocence.)

amour-propre. — Œillet. (Amour vif et pur.) — Pavot. (Sommeil.) — Rose de Provins. (Amour sacré de la patrie.)

Vigne. (Ivresse.) — Tulipe. (Magnificence.)

Fabrique d'Estampes de Gangel frères et P. Didion, à Metz. Dépôt.

example, to adopt the French interpretation of rosemary—"your presence revives me"—when fair Ophelia, in Act IV of Hamlet, identified it with "remembrance." Finally, since moral virtue was gripping Britain, English books omitted everything that might shock: heliotrope henceforth symbolized "devotion" instead of "ecstasy, I love you," which was clearly unacceptable!

Things became even more complicated—if possible—when Americans became enamored of the language of flowers. From 1850 onward, most books on floral symbolism were published in the United States. A new series of mistakes enriched the edifice still further: the vernacular names of plants are not always the same in England and America. Nor were authors of such books always botanical experts. In short, more errors crept in and, if truth be told, people fudged things so that the same flower might appear several times, under different names, in the same book. The most extraordinary thing was that each name yielded a different meaning. American authors were certainly not short on imagination.

It is easy to picture the potential misunderstandings provoked by the multiplicity of floral languages. If a French fan of Latour courted a French lady who used a bowdlerized symbolism, he was already in a tricky situation. Should he fall

"Pupils and teachers were seated in orderly fashion, each of them holding a bouquet of the prettiest and freshest springtime flowers, which perfumed the air." Thus Charlotte Brontë described a tribute to a school head in *Villette*, published in 1840. Henri-Jules-Jean Geoffroy took up the same subject in his 1893 painting, *Congratulations During School Festivities* (*above*). Children's bouquets rarely took account of the language of flowers—such complexities were reserved for adults. *Far left:* Around 1861, Lady Filmer produced this collage as a kind of riddle in which each woman is assigned a floral symbol. *Left:* A small cluster of snowdrops, signifying "hope" for the British and Americans, but "solace" for the French.

in love with an Englishwoman, his bouquets were in even deeper trouble. And should his young lady hail from Boston or New York, he would do better to give up right away. The only answer, in fact, was for a couple to agree clearly on a single reference book. Which no one did, of course, because everyone pretended to believe in an immutable, universal language of flowers, and people prided themselves on knowing the rules—even though such rules had never truly been established. Each country nevertheless forged a kind of popular consensus on the most commonly used flowers. (Even today most people are aware of the amorous connotations of red roses or the potentially unlucky associations of carnations.)

Two or three basic principles were required to avoid blunders, because tactlessness went down very poorly, as witnessed by an article published in *Le Petit Jardin* in 1902. "Although we knew that dahlias symbolize frigidity in the language of flowers, we did not know that the

courts would take it seriously. That, however, is just what happened recently in Germany. A schoolteacher hoping to enter a marriage contract ordered a bouquet costing five francs. Since roses had faded and camellias were not yet open, the florist replaced those flowers with 'white' dahlias, which angered the lady. She rejected this ambivalent compliment from her prospective husband and categorically refused the bouquet, which was returned to the florist with a refusal to pay. Hence the court case. Experts appointed by the court unanimously declared that dahlias 'have no place in a wedding bouquet.' The florist not only lost his suit but was ordered to pay court costs amounting to 375 francs." The choice of dahlias in such inappropriate circumstances represented professional negligence. Yet all the subtleties of floral savoir-faire were not necessarily mastered by what might be called "common florists" in a highly organized profession that henceforth had its lower classes and its aristocracy.

The French tradition of giving a sprig of lily-of-the-valley on 1 May as a lucky token is not completely alien to the British. In this detail of a painting (*right*) by Franz Winterhalter, titled *The First of May 1851*, the flower alludes to several festive occasions. Young Prince Arthur, shown here in the arms of his mother, Queen Victoria, was born on 1 May, as was the Duke of Wellington, here paying homage to the prince. In England, however, it is the hawthorn—or mayflower—that is most closely associated with the first of May; it was widely gathered to make up the "may pole" and to festoon interiors. *Top: Bringing in the May*, an 1862 photograph by Henry Peach Robinson. *Above: Young Girls with Roses*, another painting by Alma-Tadema in which flowers are eloquent—the artist's two daughters carry roses of life whereas their recently deceased mother in the background carries roses of mourning.

MARIUCIA
VENDITRICE
DI
FIORI
TRIESTE

GRAND FLORISTS AND
FANCY WINDOW DISPLAYS

The flower business was becoming specialized in the 1840s. There was a world of difference between a clutch of daffodils (or violets, or a potted plant), picked on the outskirts of town at dawn, and the skillful bouquets that the French called "mounted" or even "rigged." Different standards, categories, and rates applied. The hierarchy of floral "merchandise" corresponded to a hierarchy of merchants, most of whom were female, since women still largely dominated the profession. The most modest, and most picturesque, were the flower girls with their baskets. Often young and pretty—a helpful selling point—they could be found in every major city in Europe and America. With a basket attached to the waist or hanging from an elbow, they sold bouquets by chasing after hackney cabs, or proposed boutonnieres to gentlemen milling around the race track. They would also weave among the terraces of the outdoor cafés until late at night. Although illegal, this trade was tolerated, and involved only a very small selection of flowers, notably violets. Official street hawkers, meanwhile, pushed a little cart and enjoyed greater social status insofar as they had a license. Some of them sold flowers only occasionally, when prices were attractive—the next week they might be selling herrings (or perhaps both items at once). To avoid roses with a fishy smell, it was advisable to buy from specialized hawkers, recognizable by the somewhat special cart they had, equipped with a shelf for displaying bouquets. Finally, there were the settled flower ladies, who rented kiosks from the city authority. Their little trade was relatively prosperous since they enjoyed a monopoly on altar flowers, widely used in May, the month of Mary. Church flowers, in fact, were never bought from elegant flower boutiques, which regularly complained about the proximity of kiosks. Yet the extraordinary success of the elegant flower shops would suggest that the competition with kiosks did not hurt much.

Lavish bouquets bloomed everywhere in Paris. This novelty fascinated Parisians such as Paul de Kock (1793–1871), a successful vaudeville playwright, novelist, and wonderful chronicler, who wrote in the 1840s that, "we now also have very pretty and elegant shops where they sell natural flowers... These new bouquet shops are handsome in daytime and dazzling at night, for gas light gives the flowers an almost magical glow." The number of Paris boutiques grew at a prodigious rate in the last third of the century according to Henry de Vilmorin, who stated in his 1892 *Fleurs à Paris* that there were forty-five shops in 1870, and 200 twenty years later. Nor was the phenomenon limited to France, since Vilmorin noted that, "London also has many established florists in various parts of the city, for our neighbors across the channel have a highly developed taste for flowers."

The same enthusiasm reached the United States, where "Americans do not have the time to go to a market. The product has to be brought to

A Little French Flower Girl by Leopold de Moulignon (1821–97) (*above*). *Left: A Trieste Flower Seller* by Jean-François Portaels (1818–95). Ready-made bouquets were sold from baskets by "flower girls." Such bouquets might range from a simple bunch of violets to more sophisticated arrangements—in the 1850s, the most expensive kind would contain at least one large rose or camellia, filled out with pine boughs, laurustine, or orange leaves.

their doorstep. Large cities are abundantly dotted with shops devoted to selling flowers." Edith Wharton, in a short story set in the 1870s and titled *New Year's Day*, refers to a fine store on Broadway in New York: "... she paused before a florist's window, and looked appreciatively at the jars of roses and forced lilac, the compact bunches of lily-of-the-valley and violets, the first pots of close-budded azaleas. Finally she opened the shop-door, and after examining the

Jacqueminots and Marshal Niels, selected with care two perfect specimens of a new silvery-pink rose, waited for the florist to wrap them in cotton-wool, and slipped their long stems into her muff for more complete protection."

These elegant florists (note that the term "florist" was systematically applied to people who sold from a fixed shop) were much more than mere merchants. Albert Maumené, a French author who published a history of floral art in 1902, described

French painter Victor Gilbert was interested in Paris's modest flower girls, whom he depicted in the picturesque, attractive manner displayed by this *Flower Seller, Place de la Madeleine*, c. 1880 (*above*). Reality was not always so pleasant. Selling flowers in the street was the job of a horde of poor women and little girls, as seen in William Logsdail's 1888 painting of *Saint Martin-in-the-Fields* (*right*). Forced to buy their flowers as cheaply as possible, these girls came to an arrangement with the doormen of grand hotels where, every day, splendid baskets and bouquets of flowers were tossed out.

them as "fashion setters, esteemed and creative celebrities who innovate with pretty compositions, dictating and launching forms." The modern conception of the floral trade as an art had arrived. Floral artists already produced their own theorists, notably Jules Lachaume, who opened a boutique on Chaussée d'Antin in 1840, moving to 10 Rue Royale in 1897, where it still stands today. The famous firm has a fabulous history not only as florist to Napoleon III and the Romanovs, but also as the originator of the

fashion for orchids (Proust particularly liked mauve cattleyas in his buttonhole).

Lachaume's small shop was successful right from the start. He revolutionized the profession in 1847 by publishing a treatise on the art of arranging "natural" flowers. The adjective was significant, and many florists subsequently added the term "natural flowers" to their shop signs in an effort to distinguish themselves from another kind of "florist." This latter kind, typified by Lacassagne in Emile Zola's *Au Bonheur des Dames* (*Ladies Paradise*), in fact sold feathers and silk flowers. The confusion was all the greater since stores selling artificial items were almost indistinguishable from those selling the real thing. Fancy "florists" had superb window displays of ravishing compositions that looked completely real; furthermore, these elegant stores sold mainly fashion items, since decors of artificial flowers had found their way into lower-class homes and therefore had a somewhat common connotation. Given that Lachaume had decided to specialize in "the art of composing wreaths, adornments, and bouquets of all kinds for balls and parties," the border between the two spheres was very fine. Lachaume nevertheless displayed real talent and style which immediately won him the confidence of high society ladies. His treatise contained judicious advice on the harmonious balance between dress, coiffure, and the little posy held in the hand.

Lachaume's compositions were made up by Lachaume's wife, Adde, who was said to excel in such work. The situation was fairly standard for the times— stylish firms were generally headed by a man, who conceived and designed models while women actually made up the bouquets.

A picturesque scene (*top*) in which Paris street hawkers take flight at the approach of the police. *Above*: A florist in her shop, Paris, 1875. At an early date in England, at least, there were apparently floral designers who had neither shop nor stall but worked directly at their customer's premises. Henry James' *In the Cage,* a short story published in 1898, described one woman who not only managed to see high society but to enter it, becoming "mistress" of any house where bouquets needed doing.

Adde was probably assisted by numerous "lesser hands," as was the case in many other firms. A girl would begin as a "winder" (a task that involved winding a thread around flowers to bind them in clusters or set them on an artificial stem), then would move up to become successively a "binder," "wreather," and "mounter." If an assistant displayed enough taste, she might hope to become a "colorist." The ultimate promotion, however, was into "white." God-given assets—slender fingers, narrow waist, graceful neck—were required of those who worked exclusively on immaculate guelder roses, white irises, gardenias, and camellias. At that stage, a young florist might even hope to leave the workshop for the store

itself, becoming *mademoiselle la première* (First Miss). Well dressed and carefully coiffed, she would henceforth work among gleaming crystal and flowers, and would come into contact with high society—triggering all kinds of dreams.

The mirage of potential social elevation probably led to a certain kind of exploitation. Illusions loitered at the shop door in the form of young dandies or somewhat staid gentlemen whom de Kock describes as waiting for the girls to leave work. Wedding bells would never ring, however, since no nineteenth-century man of means would ever propose to a florist. Such things occurred only in books. In fact, the fictional universe of the day was full of "little flower girls" whose intrinsic

Artificial Flower Workers by Alexander Mann (1853–1908). If these workers displayed sufficient dexterity and a good sense of color, they might move from the workshop to the florist's shop. Florists also hired former hat-makers and seamstresses, as well as chambermaids with experience in arranging flowers for their mistress.

merits finally overcame class prejudice. The archetype of this persistent myth was Eliza Doolittle in George Bernard Shaw's *Pygmalion* (1913), adapted in stage and screen versions as *My Fair Lady*. Charlie Chaplin's *City Lights* also featured a blind flower girl. A few unusual cases of social success nevertheless occurred. Isabelle Brilliant was a simple street vendor who became famous in Paris during the Second Empire and was remembered for decades. She went everywhere, to the most stylish restaurants and even to the Jockey Club; the police even made an exception by officially authorizing her to sell flowers from a basket. Although she never earned a fortune, Brilliant at least managed to obtain personal fame along with a semblance of respectability. "Respectability" was what every demimonde figure sought. Zola's *Nana*, in her moments of doubt, would hark back to "her earlier, florist's ideal": a proper little life, an honest income, and a pleasant, fragrant setting. Nana, however, was not made to sell flowers, she was made to receive them by armfuls and cartloads— yet with little pleasure. What a waste.

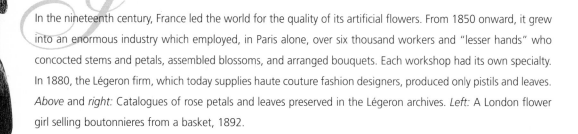

*I*n the nineteenth century, France led the world for the quality of its artificial flowers. From 1850 onward, it grew into an enormous industry which employed, in Paris alone, over six thousand workers and "lesser hands" who concocted stems and petals, assembled blossoms, and arranged bouquets. Each workshop had its own specialty. In 1880, the Légeron firm, which today supplies haute couture fashion designers, produced only pistils and leaves. *Above* and *right:* Catalogues of rose petals and leaves preserved in the Légeron archives. *Left:* A London flower girl selling boutonnieres from a basket, 1892.

GOOD BREEDING, BAD TYPES

Paul de Kock feigned puzzlement on discovering that "Parisian women consume an enormous number of bouquets, although what is strange is that these ladies buy very few themselves, and their husbands buy none at all." Florists, indeed, were probably the only people in a position to measure the true extent of the very real extramarital market. The official purchases of a married man amounted to very little, since the social contract uniting men and women in the nineteenth century left no room for passion or bouquets. A wife was not an odalisque or diva who had to be blanketed in flowers. Her husband's apparent coldness, offering her flowers only occasionally, precisely set her above all those creatures who craved constant, repeated tributes. Similarly, a married woman, if she were truly virtuous—which of course she was!—wordlessly returned bouquets sent to her by admirers. Although a gift of flowers was theoretically "inconsequential," de Kock noted that it was "highly rare that a bouquet not be followed by consequences."

Men of breeding spent money on flowers only outside the home. And it seems they spent a good deal. In 1839, the newspaper *Entracte* estimated that the average dandy disbursed 4,000 francs per year on food, 3,000 francs on theater tickets, and 1,200 francs at the florist's. And should he fall madly in love with an actress, the bill for bouquets would double or triple. Gentlemen nevertheless devoted part of their floral budget to personal use, notably for boutonnieres. The fashion of wearing a flower in the buttonhole began around 1845, when a camellia, rose, gardenia, or carnation became an elegant finishing touch to a man's evening dress. A daytime boutonniere, however, was viewed as overly foppish—in France, at least. This prejudice persisted to the end of the century, for in 1893 Charles Yriarte, author of *Les Fleurs et les Jardins de Paris*, noted that whereas highly proper Englishmen could go about their business in the morning with a flower in their lapel, it was still considered unsuitable in Paris. London's influence nevertheless encouraged many Frenchmen to sport daytime flowers, including some colorful varieties such as deep yellow Marshal Niel roses. In the evening, however, white flowers were de rigueur.

In other contexts, a boutonniere represented a profession of faith or declaration of principles. In England, a clutch of primrose pinned to the chest was a sign of membership of the Primrose League, founded in 1883 in memory of Disraeli (Queen Victoria's favorite prime minister apparently had a special penchant for that very English flower). "Political" boutonnieres, for that matter, were spreading all across Europe at that time. In Austria, for example, various parties were associated with different flowers. Stefan Zweig, in *The World of Yesterday*, notably recalled a First of May that marked the rise of the Austrian socialist party. "Workers marched in the Prater. . . with exemplary discipline, each one wearing a red carnation in his buttonhole." As soon as the red

Nineteenth-century literature contains many touching scenes involving a love letter hidden in a bouquet, such as the one being read by the young woman in Auguste Toulmouche's painting, *Billet* (*right*). It sometimes occurred, however, that the letter was never discovered, having been buried too deeply among the densely packed flowers. Alphonse Karr, in his 1858 *Voyage autour de mon Jardin* (*Trip Around My Garden*), recounts just such a tale: a delightful old lady unknots a bouquet of dried flowers that she had carefully preserved for nearly half a century, only to discover—at last!—the heart-felt declaration she had awaited in vain. *Above:* A Londoner does her Christmas shopping in Harrod's flower department, 1902.

carnation "made its appearance as a party emblem… another flower began to appear in buttonholes, the white carnation, the sign of membership in the Christian Social party!" Soon a third flower appeared, namely "the blue cornflower, Bismarck's favorite flower and the emblem of the German National Party."

Men thus sported flowers as a statement of elegance or politics when going about their business—or pleasure. That, however, was another story. The favors of a fashionable courtesan could not be won with a simple gardenia or clutch of violets. Possessing one of those voluptuous creatures necessarily meant smothering her with flowers. They provided a way for her to assess a gentleman's wealth and anticipate subsequent gains. Zola's Nana, for that matter—to return to France's legendary concubine—used precisely this method to select her lovers, thereby "creating a continuous catastrophe of flowers around her." Her comments left no doubt on this score. "Well then, if Rose wants Léon, she can have him. For what he's worth. One bouquet a week, if that!" Nana clearly did not like flowers in themselves—

At Dawn by Belgian painter Charles Hermans (1838–1924) shows a tipsy gentleman emerging from a night of revelry with women on his arms, boutonniere askew, and the evening's bouquets scattered in the gutter. This disreputable figure recalls the individuals associated with Zola's *Nana*: "He was a skirt-chaser who ate up his fortune with sordid women; he lacked any moral sense and profited from the wealth of others, paying for a bouquet or a meal only every now and then."

bouquets piled up in her antechamber and her carriage without winning so much as a glance from her. What she liked about the orgy of flowers was the tribute they represented from men burning with desire, the price men were ready to pay. When men no longer paid up, and when creditors began knocking at the door, the bouquets that a few faithful companions continued to send Nana became irritatingly pointless. The scullery maids in the kitchen muttered what even their mistress was beginning to think—too bad

these expensive bouquets cannot even be parlayed into ten centimes.

Another fictional heroine of French literature had preceded Nana in her floral debauch, namely Marguerite Gautier, Alexandre Dumas' *Dame aux Camélias*. She, too, was responsible for "expenditures on bouquets greater than those required to allow an entire family to live happily." A closer look at the lady's fine camellias reveals that her interest in flowers was also highly "professional." The inevitable bouquet of camellias that accompanied her to a ball or the theater was thus white twenty-five days of the month, red the other five days. Dumas, who offered no explicit explanation, was clearly dissembling when he declared that he "never knew the reason for the change in color." The story nevertheless has Marguerite reject her lover on a "red bouquet" evening. He is advised to return the next evening, when the camellias will have turned white. Ultimately, Marguerite Gautier's flowers were rather vulgar.

Madame Roche playing the lead role in *La Dame aux Camélias* (*above*). The "Lady of the Camellias" was not the only person to appreciate camellias, which were at the height of their popularity in the 1850s due to the regular shape of their blooms, their propensity to blossom in winter, and their lack of scent (which meant that they could be used on all occasions). Fifty years later, however, camellias were out of fashion for the same reasons that had led to their popularity. The bloom was considered too heavy and was criticized for lacking fragrance! *Vignettes:* Camellias illustrated by Mrs Withers, c. 1830.

At the other end of society, well-bred ladies cultivated different floral habits, except when it came to public receptions—balls and parties—where women were uniformly bedecked in flowers. Charles Worth, who pioneered the idea of haute couture on both sides of the Atlantic, produced the sublime and voluminous ball gowns of the 1860s that were trimmed with large bunches of fresh flowers from bust to train. Although these spectacular floral effects became somewhat more subdued in subsequent years, elegant young ladies still flaunted accessories such as a sprig of wisteria on the shoulder (caressing the bare arm), a plume of lily-of-the-valley and feathers in the hair, a cluster of roses on the breast, or a velvet collar stitched with Parma violets. Then there were the posies carried by young women in Victorian England, matching the rest of their attire. By mid-century, these posies were being carried in tiny holders, which themselves became exquisite and expensive objects. They might be shaped as a cone or a horn of plenty, made of gold, mother-of-pearl, silver-gilt, or ivory, and set with pearls, turquoise, or gems. And since ladies never abandoned their bouquets during the entire evening—any more than they would a fan—ingenious devices were invented. Some bouquet holders were equipped with a chain and a ring that went

on the finger, so that the flowers could be dropped while waltzing, and immediately picked up again. Others contained a moveable tripod system that could be momentarily placed on a table. Finally, some were amusingly set with a miniature device that was nothing less than a rear-view mirror: while pretending to smell her bouquet, a lady could take a glance without being seen. Young women could thus assess the looks they were receiving, while older ladies could keep an eye on their daughters and potential suitors.

These balls, with their low necklines and floral accouterments, were considered legitimate sites of seduction, since a match would conform to the young lady's station. The outcome was supposed to be a wedding ceremony, the apotheosis of an honest women and the sole occasion on which a lady of breeding could be smothered in bouquets without fearing for her reputation. A few rules had to be respected however, and all these rules—from the color of the petals to the choice of compositions—were codified in books of etiquette.

The long parade of nuptial flowers began with the proposal. A few hours after a young man's request for her hand had been accepted, a florist delivered the first—immaculately white—bouquet. On the first day of the engagement, the

It was not considered seemly for a woman to appear in public with nothing in her hands. This meant that little bouquets, fans, and evening bags became essential accessories at a ball. Flowers had the drawback, however, of soiling gloves, and it was perhaps for that reason that bouquet-holders were invented. Such holders ultimately became precious objects in their own right. *Above* and *top:* Various flower-holders produced between 1830 and 1900. *Right:* Women with flowers on gowns and in hair during a *Party* depicted by Jean Béraud (1849–36).

arrival of the prospective husband was preceded by a fine basket of flowers. The delivery of flowers then continued every day until the wedding itself. No lapses were tolerated. The litany of roses, guelder roses, violets, and white lilacs came to an end only on the day of the ceremony, when the groom made a final present of flowers. On the continent, this meant a basket of flowers, whereas English brides received a bouquet, thereby launching the tradition of walking down the aisle with a profuse, and sometimes vast, bouquet in hand.

A different innovation swept France, where the bride wore orange blossom as a tiara in her hair, as a corsage, or at her waist. This custom was relatively recent, as was the wearing of a white gown, which became standard only during the nineteenth century. Paris was the only city in Europe to boast a horticulturist who grew fine orange blossoms all year round. From the 1860s onward, Parisian brides could wear tiaras of fresh orange blossoms, mounted on silver wire, even in winter.

Once the wedding was over, a well-bred lady had to renounce such floral display. Of course, she received bouquets on New Year's Day, when gentlemen who had been invited to dine at her home during the year showed their appreciation with a gift of flowers or confectionery. Similarly, for grand receptions, she might pin fresh blossoms in her hair or on her bodice. But for everyday wear, and on the little straw hat worn in spring after Easter Monday, she had the good sense to wear only silk flowers. Silk flowers were less messy, and did not stain fabrics or ribbons. They were a sign of thrift and simplicity, two key virtues that became a mark of distinction for women. Bourgeois ideology glorified women with domestic qualities, which were best displayed in the proper management of a fine home—one full of flowers.

Signing the Register, by Edmund Blair Leighton (1853–1922) (*above*). *Left: The Morning of the Wedding*, by Carl Herpfer (1836–97). Only brides from affluent families could afford to wear fresh orange flowers on their wedding day—it was a costly extravagance that uncles traditionally offered their nieces. Less wealthy brides had to settle for artificial orange flowers, which were then preserved under glass.

FLOWERS IN THE HOME

Domestic life in the second half of the nineteenth century would have been unthinkable without an abundance of vegetation. Elegant salons almost resembled indoor gardens—daylight filtered through windows screened by large pink hydrangeas and arabesques of ivy, while boxes on legs of rattan or ironwork held flowering plants. The 1850s favored potfuls of azaleas, rhododendrons, camellias, myrtle, and pomegranate, but by the 1880s people began to prefer baskets arranged with ferns, palm shoots, and crotons. All flowers and plants were potted, since cut flowers were too ephemeral and costly to constitute part of the everyday setting. With no one to appreciate them, they would have seemed wasteful, violating the sacrosanct principle of thriftiness. This was clearly not the case, however, when the mistress of the house was receiving at home. On the day of the week when she received callers, she enlivened her sitting room with fresh, fragrant flowers. As Yriarte pointed out, a "salon without flowers was offensive to the eye, an indignity for the woman."

In all good households, however, it was the formal dinner—for which guests received an invitation card—that provided an occasion for a veritable floral event. Hostesses mobilized all their faculties of organization and domestic ceremony for the occasion. Table settings required such a grand display of flowers that they constituted the largest single source of income for florists—apart from funeral wreaths. This phenomenon occurred when dining "à la Russe" became fashionable: whereas French tradition called for steaming soup and vegetable tureens to be placed on the table when the guests arrived, Russian-style service entailed bringing plates of food from the kitchen and setting one in front of each diner, as is still done today. The space on the table previously reserved for serving dishes was allotted, around 1845, to baskets and "table ends" of ivy, periwinkle, and laurel mounted with

In the Conservatory, by James Tissot (1836–1902) (*above*). *Left: A Fashionable Lady*, by Firmin Baes (1874–1945). The use of flowers was supposed to remain moderate, even if they gave great pleasure. It was rare for the mistress of a house to overdo bouquets, except for special occasions, as suggested in *Elisabeth et son Jardin Allemand* (1898) by Elisabeth von Arnim: "Oh those shrubs of lilac! I picked countless bunches, and there is not a pot, not a bowl, not a bucket in the house that is not filled with their purple splendor. The servants seem very agitated, convinced that a grand reception is in the works, while I run from room to room to enjoy the sight."

multicolored blooms. Parisian hostesses also liked dahlias with round flowers, which were so appreciated during the reign of Louis-Philippe. Such arrangements were rather stiff and large, becoming positively bloated in 1865, when large centerpieces became so outsized that they had to be delivered on long barrows. Since such arrangements also grew in height, guests could no longer see the person opposite, which hindered conversation considerably.

English tables, meanwhile, were decorated completely differently, being more refined and more convivial. Back in the eighteenth century, the English developed an original approach by inventing a special type of centerpiece, called an epergne (subsequently adopted only in the United States, despite its French origin). An epergne is a centerpiece of precious metal or porcelain composed of a variable number of branched bowls or baskets rising from a central base. The object itself is therefore already a kind of bouquet, and it is hardly surprising that, although initially filled fruit and sweets, epergnes were ultimately adorned with small bunches of flowers. Then the bowls evolved into vases, placed at various angles and levels, blossoming into a multiple bouquet holder. Epergnes retained an airy quality that was pleasant

to behold without blocking the gaze—clusters of roses or violets would gracefully hover in the air, especially once glass and crystal were used to emphasize the transparency of these fine objects. In the simpler models produced in the nineteenth century, the epergne's vases took the form of small funnels, as seen in the color plates of publications like Mrs. Beeton's famous 1859 *Book of Household Management*. Beeton proposed a range of table settings that, apart from certain lavish arrangements, invariably repeated the theme of a central bouquet or epergne matched by individual vases in front of each guest.

The English were nevertheless capable of more surprising settings. Other household manuals—of

Ferdinand George Waldmüller's painting of a magnificent German table decoration from the first half of the nineteenth century, titled *Birthday Table* (*right*), illustrates more concern for artistic impact than for ease of conversation. English hostesses, in contrast, did their utmost to reconcile both aspects of the problem, as illustrated in a dinner table "à la Russe" (*top*) shown in the 1890 publication *Everyday Cookery*. Festoons of flowers are raised or broken in strategic places to enable guests to chat with the person opposite. *Above:* A plate from a Victorian catalogue advertising several kinds of flower-bearing centerpiece called "epergnes."

which there were countless examples in England and elsewhere—suggested floral extravagances within reach of any moderately affluent and painstaking hostess. A three-tiered tray, for instance, could be stacked with greenery, violets, and water lilies, the whole thing being topped by a block of ice. During the meal, the ice would slowly melt and dribble among the flowers, like a real spring. French hostesses, who had scorned English epergnes, succumbed to these watery displays in the late nineteenth century, when they also adopted the understated richness of the English "parterre"—an oval, square, or diamond-shaped sheet of moss stuck with flowerets and tiny ferns. It is impossible to list all the English trends imported by the French, giving their tables a more natural, modest feel. Such sobriety, however, was not solely a question of aesthetics; Englishwomen, much more than their continental sisters, associated flowers with virtuousness, which precluded excesses and wastefulness.

Indeed flowers were endowed with a moralizing, socializing mission. British workers, apparently, would turn away from pub doors if only their wives were wise enough to have flowers at home—a domestic bouquet "purified the atmosphere of slums and triggered a sense of well-being." English ladies indulged in floral proselytism, distributing bouquets to housewives in London's seedy districts. One might wonder about the kind of welcome they received, but it was reported to be excellent, even enthusiastic. Similar operations were therefore conducted in the United States on an even larger scale. An article in the Parisian newspaper *Le Matin* recounted an experiment in New York around 1880. The local press appealed to New York residents lucky enough to have a country home to send bunches of daisies to decorate working-class tenements. On the appointed day, "the streets were jammed with delivery vehicles bringing bunches, cases, and barrels of flowers." Reporters and health department doctors took care of distributing the flowers, aided by police. The neighborhood was overjoyed, and quarreling Italians even stopped fighting in order to create some order around the bouquets.

Convinced by social crusaders or—more probably—concerned to imitate the affluent classes, mistresses of modest households ultimately began decorating their homes in flowers. By the end of the nineteenth century, every welcoming household had a little bouquet in the middle of the family table. A bouquet symbolized a certain idea of happiness. And, above all, it was no longer an extravagance—horticulture had been making considerable progress in the meantime, placing cut flowers within the reach of almost every pocketbook.

The *Art du Bouquet*, published in 1913 by a certain N.C. Clairoix, was one of several highly popular French books on the subject. The author claimed that she became an expert in floral art by not hesitating "to take off [her] rings and care for the flowers." Not all ladies did so—Madame Clairoix complained that "arranging bouquets is too often left to the servants." The simplest thing for the mistress of the house was to decorate the home with potted flowers, as suggested by Gustav Wilhem Blom's late nineteenth-century painting of *Figures with a Bowl of White Chrysanthemums* (above). True artistry, on the other hand, went into the vase carried by the *Girl with Sunflowers* (1889) by Danish painter Michael Ancher (left).

TRAINS OF ROSES

Paris was caught out by the extraordinary boom in the flower trade. A large new market hall completed around 1870, Les Halles de Baltard, did not even include a section for flower stalls; twenty years later, growers and wholesalers were loudly demanding their own market. Meanwhile, the flower market in central Paris, which had become the largest in the world, continued to operate in a drafty, open space squeezed between the butter and poultry pavilion and the seafood pavilion. In contrast, London's Covent Garden had a fine building devoted solely to the flower market, although the allotted space was already overflowing

with bunches and buckets when Oscar Wilde published *The Picture of Dorian Gray* in 1890. Traffic was bustling and dense, and in the early hours of the morning Dorian encountered "huge carts filled with nodding lilies," and lines of "boys carrying crates of striped tulips, and of yellow and red roses" as they threaded their way "through the huge jade-green piles of vegetables."

Suddenly supplies of flowers swelled to proportions unthinkable prior to 1850, when flowers continued to arrive at markets as they always had. Ever since Renaissance chaplet-makers had set up outside city walls, major European towns were ringed by green suburbs where, every night, hordes of gardeners would set off for the market

The woman who has just purchased flowers at the Hojbroplads flower market in Copenhagen, as depicted by Paul Fischer, climbs into an automobile that sports a little vase with flowers. Once upon a time the interiors of luxury trains, cabs, and cars all boasted bouquets in small conical vases affixed to the side, a practice that survived up to the Second World War. Elisabeth Taylor's novel, *Angel*, describes a woman who drove around in a dark red Fiat decorated with not only silk tassels and knobs, but also vases of roses and maidenhair fern.

with loads of greenery or bunches of pansies, mignonette, and roses. More or less the same thing occurred in the United States, even though floral traditions were obviously more recent—green belts existed in New York and New Jersey, where the early Dutch colonists had exported their know-how long ago.

In short, the market remained a local one. Suburban production met the town-dwellers' needs. As soon as the sun rose, the green belt around Paris bloomed in unison—gardeners from Ivry and Montrouge hauled hyacinths, tulips, and tuberoses to Les Halles, whereas Fontenay-sous-Bois supplied primroses and cineraria. At Bourg-la-Reine, Clamart, and Verrières, growers "did"

Parma violets. This pertained to the warm months, obviously, since despite the existence of greenhouses, the winter months were hard to bridge—florists' displays suffered as soon as the first heavy frosts hit, even as prices spiraled sharply upward.

While Paris was blanketed in snow, however, the French Riviera from Menton to Toulon was enjoying an endless spring. That was where Alphonse Karr, a polemical journalist and former editor of *Le Figaro* newspaper, set up shop in 1853. Forced into exile for political reasons, he finally settled in Nice, which was still under Italian control. Karr was drawn by the warm climate, and intended to become an enthusiastic gardener

J.W. Joy's *Bayswater Omnibus* (1895) (*above*) shows a Londoner laden with a bouquet of roses, apparently picked from the garden rather than bought at a florist's or a market. Commercial bouquets of the day were round, dense, and wrapped in white paper, as indicated in Victor Gilbert's 1880 painting of a *Flower Market*, probably set in Paris (*following pages*).

during his forced vacation. He was astonished to discover the horticultural ignorance of a region with such fine weather and profuse wild flowers. Moreover, when denizens of Nice wanted a bouquet, they ordered it from Genoa, receiving what Karr described as "a tray of squeezed, heaped, packed, misshapen flowers." Karr began to realize that enough varieties of flowers could be grown in Nice—outdoors and in all seasons—to fill the winter gap of French horticulturists. He therefore rented a large garden and imported samples—from France, Belgium, and Italy—of all the plants he wished to introduce. After a year of work, his plots were already fulfilling their promise. Highly encouraged, Karr decided to open a shop. But first he ordered several bouquets from the best Parisian florists in order to study their "manner," which he then adapted with a

great deal of taste and "a freedom that allowed the flowers to retain their shape, bearing, and air of contentment." Success was immediate, and all the rich foreigners vacationing on the Riviera began buying their bouquets from Karr. More important, they sent his flowers everywhere—to Paris, London, Berlin, and Saint Petersburg. These days, it is hard to imagine the wonder aroused in 1860 by the arrival in a Paris home of a large bouquet from Monsieur Karr's Nice establishment—a profuse bouquet with a scent of orange flowers that caressed your face as soon as the thin wooden crate was opened, bringing summer sunshine with it. These flowers provided a wonderful boost for Mediterranean tourism, as well as a rousing cheer for southern horticulture.

Soon the Riviera was shipping chilly Paris all its finest mimosas, saffron roses, hyacinths,

These two Seeberger photographs document the flower show held in the Bois de Boulogne, Paris, in June 1909. An article in *Le Monde Illustré* reported the event and mentioned the winners of the "decorated carriage" contest: "The grand prize went to Madame Suzanne Murat, ensconced in a delightful hackney cab bedecked in daisies and carnations tied with gauze. Other prize ribbons went to Madames Gaby Nellys and Melza, gracefully charming in a black landau garlanded with daisies, and to Madames Coll and De la Vallette, in a double phaeton bearing pretty girls among the peonies."

mignonettes, carnations, and lilac heathers, not to mention the small ready-made bouquets produced at Solliès-Pont. This winter and spring supply would be replaced by "Paris" (as all flowers produced in the capital region are still called today) in late May, when southern roses began wilting under the heat. All of this was made possible, of course, by the development of the railroads. By 1911, special trains laden exclusively with flowers were making the trip up to Paris.

The capital's own flowers also began traveling by train. Starting in 1860, suburbanites who took the line from Vincennes into Bastille after midnight would see the 12:45 a.m. arrival of the famous "rose train" that brought flowers from Brie-Comte-Robert into Les Halles. Southern competition, in fact, had spurred local horticulture and the forced flowering of fashionable varieties. Some twenty wholesale gardens around Paris began producing lilacs, and an equal number grew roses (which were subject to a number of refined tortures and deprivations designed to make them blossom at will, all year round). These local flowers were much more expensive than the Riviera's outdoor products, but they were just as beautiful and highly sought after.

The same trend occurred everywhere flowers were appreciated. In the 1890s, hundreds of thousands of forced roses bloomed in New York greenhouses, while cultivators planted acres of gladioli, tuberoses, and lilies. French production and trade developed with the same

impetuousity as other national industries. In England, meanwhile, railroads enabled distant regions to compete with flowers from the green belt around London—the first daffodils from the Scilly Isles arrived in Covent Garden in 1867. London florists also imported hothouse specimens from the Paris area, notably Versailles, whose flowers were highly valued. France, meanwhile, sought supplies from Ghent, Belgium, where remarkable azaleas and orchids were being produced. Nor was distant Russia excluded from floral exchange—the long Moscow winter was warmed by bouquets from Nice.

The flower trade had already become international. As Charles Yriarte remarked in 1893, the days were over when people "swooned at the sight of a bouquet of roses in January." Almost anything could be had at any time of the year. Supplies were plentiful, fortunately, since a new rage for flower festivals and decorated carriages took root in Cannes and Nice. By the end of the nineteenth century, this type of celebration marked the start of the summer season everywhere socialites gathered, especially in Paris where various flower shows were held in June at the Tuileries Gardens, the Longchamp racecourse, and the Bois de Boulogne. Parades of horse-drawn carriages enabled people to admire "a most delightfully decorated landau," a "double phaeton bearing pretty girls among the peonies," or a "victoria adorned with feathery asparagus fronds and cattleyas in pretty shades of mauve."

*I*n many French spas and holiday resorts, flower festivals dating back to the late nineteenth century remain the year's big event even today. In Luchon, for example, this tradition has survived for over one hundred years, as witnessed by the first poster announcing the event in 1890 (*above*), by famous lithographer Jules Chéret. *Right* (*clockwise from top left*): Paul Nadar's photograph of an elegant lady smelling a bouquet—of *silk* flowers; Ballerina Anna Pavlova buried under flowers at the Ritz Hotel, 1912; two Americans in front of one of the floral extravaganzas that were so popular around 1900—it is hard to tell whether the flowers are designed for a celebration or a funeral; an American bride and groom posing under a traditional bell of flowers.

THE BENEFICIAL INFLUENCE
OF JAPANESE BOUQUETS

Florists became intoxicated by the profusion of flowers henceforth available to them, and by the public esteem they enjoyed. They wanted to give free reign to their expressiveness beyond the confines of their workshops, just as a painter or sculptor would do. Starting in the 1890s, florists began exhibiting their creations at contests of floral arrangements. For better or (sometimes) worse, groups of amateurs, generally upper class and idle ladies, entered these events. But these ladies at least deserve credit for launching such contests, in which professional florists had not initially participated. The first competition, organized in England in 1861 by the Royal Horticultural Society, was non-professional and almost exclusively female. The jury included the Countess of Shelburne, the Countess of Ducie, Lady Marianne Alford, and Lady Middleton. Other ladies battled it out for the top prize—which was nevertheless won by a man, a certain Thomas C. March of the Lord Chamberlain's office.

By the late nineteenth century, these contests had spread to all kinds of floral exposition throughout Europe. Amateurs continued to compete in their own category, but were soon eclipsed by professional florists who would go to any length to add another medal to their collection, recreating pastoral scenes complete with thatched cottage or mill buried under waves of clematis, or magnificently decorating a salon with table settings and candelabra. Although spectacular, such displays were not very innovative. French florists in particular tended to rest on their laurels. The Belgians were more dynamic—the Ghent horticultural school offered its first courses in flower arranging in 1897, well ahead of France. Germany, meanwhile, was in full creative swing, publishing Europe's only specialist review where, three times a month, florists exchanged views and presented photographs of their latest creations. Given this spirit of rivalry, Germans perfected their technical skills—which remain remarkable to this day—and undertook bold experiments, being among the first to explore the possibilities of cactus dahlias, chrysanthemums, and irises. These sinuous, tangled flowers were reputed to be difficult, yet they suddenly came to the fore around 1890 when the Western art of flower arranging encountered Japanese bouquets. When comparing the two, Western-style compositions did not come off very well—everyone realized how profuse and tightly packed they were, as though "passed through a hydraulic compressor." Pierre Loti's famous 1888 novel, *Madame Chrysanthème*, described the delicate floral arrangements produced by his petite Japanese wife, reminding him "with a certain irony of the big, round cauliflower-shaped bouquets produced by our florists in France, wrapped in lace or white paper."

French Glassmaker Emile Gallé (in an 1892 portrait by Victor Prouvé) was famous for his fine vases with floral patterns. Gallé's designs were directly inspired by nature, and he kept in close touch with horticulturists, notably Victor Lemoine. Like Gallé, Lemoine was from Nancy, and was not only one of the first growers to cultivate large hybrid gladioli in magnificent colors, but he also created the double-flowered white lilac.

Peonies (c. 1895), by American artist William Merritt Chase (1849–1916). The Japanese flavor of this painting was widespread in the West, revolutionizing attitudes toward bouquets, as reflected by French writer Pierre Loti in *Madame Chrysanthème* : "Our place resembles a Japanese image—nothing but small screens, small bizarre stools holding vases with bouquets and, in the back of the apartment, an altar-like niche with a large gilded Buddha majestically seated on a lotus."

The English and Americans felt the same way. Isabella Bird, in *Unbeaten Tracks in Japan*, published in London in 1881, castigated Western bouquets for the grotesque, barbaric way they systematically destroyed the grace and individuality of each flower.

First-rate florists ultimately caught on. They steadily replaced mounted pieces with airy,

emergence of "modern," slender roses with pointed buds. Although not yet the starved, stubbornly closed "Baccarat" rose of the twentieth century, the new roses heralded the flowers and arrangements that radically altered public taste for decades.

This ascetic tendency, fueled by Japonism, transformed interior decoration. Proust, in *In a*

supple bouquets of stemmed flowers that rose vertically, acquiring greater beauty in the transparency of crystal vases. In the same spirit, greenery no longer simply masked gaps or imperfections but was used to soften and add suppleness, leading to the widely noted introduction of gauzy, feathery asparagus. Another innovation that soon became classic was the large bouquet of roses. Roses, too, had changed. The introduction and cross-breeding of tea-scented China roses (later called "tea roses") led in the 1860s to the

Budding Grove, compared Odette Swann's salon in the 1880s to its transformation ten years later. The original salon was a particularly dense and crowded "indoor garden." By 1890, however, it contained only a few floral decorations, "a rose or an iris from Japan in a long-necked crystal vase that could not contain so much as one more flower." Odette, however, was part of a social set thoroughly conversant with the latest fashion. In other circles, even refined ones, her bouquets would still have seemed austere. Many florists,

Jan Voerman's late nineteenth-century painting of *Two Glasses with White Roses* features a modern variety of rose. In 1867 there appeared a variety of rose dubbed "La France," the first in a long line of modern roses with long, pointed buds which transformed Western bouquets (previously containing only round roses). This type of flower resulted from hybrids with Chinese varieties known as "tea roses" due to their fragrance. It is not known whether the scent was natural or came from the chests of tea in which the first Chinese roses were imported.

including the finest, were not convinced that such a spare setting was required. Floral art in the late nineteenth century also embraced harps, lyres, imitation artist's easels, and huge eggs all made of flowers, not to mention feather doves stuck into baskets, clouds of tulle swathed around wicker-work, and ribbons everywhere. These were the forms in which flowers remained most popular and widely known. People seem to have learned only technical virtuosity from the Japanese, overlooking the main point—naturalism.

Naturalism meant breathing space, and above all a little spontaneity. This could be found only among the artists and poets where, for that matter, Japonism first took root, and where ready-made ideas—and ready-made bouquets—had long been viewed with suspicion. Literature and the arts produced not just new floral aesthetes and theorists but also veritable "bouquet artists." Hans Christian Andersen, for example, had the same fondness for wild plants as he did for little mermaids and match girls. One wonders what Danish ladies of the 1860s, accustomed to splendid baskets of hothouse flowers, thought when they received the bouquets Andersen sent them—simple, unconventional, and sometimes almost wilted. The open-minded Andersen liked faded flowers. In England, Oscar Wilde also liked to do what wasn't done. He exhibited horrendous, anachronistic taste in 1875 when he decorated his rooms at Oxford with blue China vases (which

subsequently came back into fashion). These porcelain vases appear on the mantelpiece in *The Picture of Dorian Gray*, filled with parrot tulips. Bouquets of tulips were a novelty, for the flower had long been relegated to pots, its stems being considered too long and bare for vases.

Nor did tulips figure much in paintings. The nineteenth century produced countless flower paintings, a veritable flood of conventional compositions which, at least until the 1860s, remained unimaginatively pretty yet sold well among an appreciative general public. Floral pieces nevertheless helped to revive flowers once again, giving them new vigor and naturalness, when it came to work by the likes of Vincent van Gogh who, freeing himself from traditional depictions, exploited a richly colorful palette in such dazzling subjects as his large *Sunflowers*. His use of a single variety of flowers was on the cutting edge of modernism, as was monochrome composition. There was nothing cute or pretty in his majestic, gold-maned sunflowers. Nor was there anything conventional in the sixteen wonderful flower paintings into which Manet poured his final energy from 1881 until his death in 1883. The sick artist rarely left his studio, where friends consoled him with gifts of flowers—a sprig of lilac, two or three peonies, a small bunch of roses. These gifts were not so much bouquets as a sign of affection, a breath of fresh air, a little jolt of life. Which is just how Manet painted them—exactly as they were,

Edouard Manet's *Pinks and Clematis in a Crystal Vase*, c. 1882. Manet was too much of a dandy to do his own gardening. He was more familiar with fashionable Parisian bouquets than with flowerbeds. The flowers he painted in the last three years of his life reflected the vogue for corsages: small compositions arranged by a tasteful female friend or by the florists frequented by his elegant visitors. Yet at the end of his life, these simple and moving flowers are stripped of all worldliness.

drinking water from an ordinary glass or a simple crystal vase. Henri Fantin-Latour's arrangements were perhaps less moving, yet also testify to a profound search for authenticity. He tried to be "as true and sincere as possible," and above all to remain simple, like his artistic mentor, Chardin. Fantin-Latour rediscovered the tousled charm of small eighteenth-century bouquets, freshly and cheaply picked in the garden. It was too late, however. Critics were no longer interested in paintings that took flowers as their subject. They had seen it all already.

The same feeling prevailed among interior decorators. No flowery prose came from Edith Wharton when she published *The Decoration of Houses* in New York in 1897. Criticizing the tendency to accumulate, she exhorted women to rid themselves of everything superfluous. Let them put all their bric-à-brac, including vases, back into the attic. They should forget their enthusiasm for flowered wallpaper and chintz, which only collected dust. Entrance halls should be free of plants, tables rid of bouquets. Not a single flower should remain. Yet that was precisely how flowers held out—singly, perched high on a stem in a tubular vase. Single-flower vases, first glimpsed in Odette Swann's salon, were manufactured by the thousands in the 1920s. This represented a strange, unprecedented development in the

history of Western bouquets—at no other time was a single bloom considered a complete decor in itself. To a certain extent, this special arrangement ennobled flowers through a "solitaire" setting—like diamonds.

Single-flower vases also provided a pause for reflection. They lasted just long enough for flowers to establish themselves on long stems, to recover their naturalism. Profusion then came roaring back. In 1925, F. Scott Fitzgerald had *The Great Gatsby* order a veritable flower show for his meeting with Daisy, along with countless recipients to contain everything. This was also the period when American florists launched the slogan, "Say it with flowers."

In Europe, meanwhile, the Dutch were preparing a veritable revolution. It almost went unnoticed, since it took place in the café where growers from the small town of Aalsmeer, outside Amsterdam, used to meet. The candles on the tables and the lively conversations harked back to the old days of "tulipomania." This time, however, minds and goals were clear: Dutch bulb growers were tired of being at the mercy of individual buyers. They therefore founded, in 1912, the first flower auction. Western bouquets were moving into a new age. Aalsmeer would slowly become to flowers what Chicago is to wheat. Stem by stem, the floral trade was about to sweep the planet.

Flowers were reinterpreted in a stylized, brightly colored way by the decorative movement of the 1920s. They also became the subject of fanciful graphic works like this watercolor of *Mixed Flowers* (*above*) by Scottish designer Charles Rennie Mackintosh, painted in France in 1925. Among the forget-me-nots, cornflowers, geraniums, pinks, and campanula are several flowers in the upper left that metamorphose into birds. *Right:* In Catherine B. Gulley's *Memories*, dated 1924, real anemones in the bouquet harmonize with flowers printed on the dress.

Flower
Markets

If there is one thing in the recent history of flowers that has barely changed, it must be the markets. Although flower markets now offer more varieties and colors than in the nineteenth century, they still feature the same stalls, stacks of bunches, and large buckets of cool water from which thirsty flowers drink. Specialist markets are one of the most charming attractions of European capitals, even if the flowers themselves have become disappointingly standardized ever since Holland began flooding the world with its "ready-made" bouquets— a sprig of gypsophila and four colorful blooms wrapped in a cone of printed or festooned paper. These fairground bouquets are the worst things the Dutch ever invented. Yet the Dutch are also the only merchants to offer, on the same stand and at practically the same prices, both brightly colored and subtle flowers that are unavailable on the markets of other countries. Fabulous pickings are to be had on the barges docked along the Singel canal in Amsterdam, one of Europe's most famous markets, if not the prettiest. Alongside rather gaudy, touristy bric-à-brac, outstanding varieties are sold at very attractive prices, especially during the bulb season from March to May. Shoppers can treat themselves to the rare pleasure of a large bouquet of tuberoses, or even crown imperials, which other continental florists rarely use as cut flowers. Singel also bursts with bouquets of amaryllis and more familiar bunches of fleshy hyacinths (white, pink, and

Delft blue), which made the leap from potted plants to stem flowers several years ago. Although affordable in Amsterdam, cut hyacinths remain a luxury on Paris markets.

It is perhaps worth dwelling on Paris's "flower markets"—or what remains of them. There were eleven at the turn of the twentieth century, most having been established around 1870. Many more than elsewhere in Europe, they ensured that the image of a romantic and bohemian Paris was durably linked to its flowery stalls. They are still part of the capital's reputation, especially in North America where "flower markets" hold an exotic appeal, U.S. cities being singularly devoid of them. The more prosaic reality is that Paris now has only three markets.

First comes the oldest, the Quai aux Fleurs, with its typical nineteenth-century cast-iron architecture. It offers potted flowers and bedding plants, but few cut flowers, which were never its specialty. The Madeleine market, founded in 1834, is something else again. That is where stylish Parisian ladies used to go to buy their bouquets. It is not worth dwelling on the current fate of this market, unfortunately disfigured by roadworks. There remains the market at Place des Ternes, established somewhat later. It presents a pleasant mosaic of colors, but is not a place for bargains or new discoveries. Parisian flower markets cultivate the traditional, picturesque side of their local image, for which there is obviously something to be said.

All kinds of flower market exist, each one different from the others. The term includes open markets which generally sell flowers in bunches, as seen at the Singel market in Amsterdam (*right*, clockwise from top left): a display of roses, irises, ivy, and blue delphiniums; buckets of daffodils, gerbera, and sweet peas; bunches of freesias; varieties of ranunculus. Other flower markets, or "halls," are reserved exclusively for trade professionals—the general public is not allowed to make purchases (except at Covent Garden in London, where both old and new markets have always been open to all). *Above: Covent Garden*, English school, 1930. *Previous pages:* Covent Garden flower market—portrait of a merchant in 1950 (*left*), and the flower stalls as they appeared in 1925 (*right*).

Other French cities also boast charming, semi-permanent displays of flowers. Towns in Provence have the advantage of the proximity of gardens and greenhouses in the Var region, which produce 35 per cent of France's total output. In recent years, the town of Hyères has become a regional flower hub, with a vast, shiny new trade complex for wholesale distribution. Strangely enough, however, the city itself has only one flower market for the local population, which is held only one Sunday per month. At Aix-en-Provence, on the other hand, the local flower market is a regular pleasure. It operates three times per week on the square in front of the town hall, whose fine seventeenth-century facade is abundantly carved with festoons of flowers and fruit, baroque scrolls and blossoms. In Nice, meanwhile, thousands of flowers perfume Cours Saleya every day of the week except

Monday. Nice was long the undisputed center of Mediterranean horticulture until Hyères began to compete for the title. Nice retains its glamor, however, and some Paris professionals still refer to all Mediterranean production as "Nice." Its flower market features all the varieties which were local curiosities until not very long ago, being picked the eve or very day of sale. These include mimosa, which flowered for the first time in Cannes in 1880, and honey-scented yellow everlasting (*Helichrisum*), first commercially cultivated back in the nineteenth century by growers in Ollioules, making several of them rich. Then there are dense bunches of violets, grown among the olive trees in Tourette-sur-Loup, France's own "violet capital," well ahead of Toulouse. Even today, an armful of flowers bought on Cours Saleya is perhaps the finest souvenir of a trip to Nice.

Professional gardeners cutting snapdragons (*top*) and strelitzia in greenhouses in Antibes (*above*). *Right:* Audrey Hepburn makes a more theatrical harvest in this shot from the American musical, *Funny Face* (1956). Hepburn was obviously fated for floral roles—in 1964 she played an unforgettable Eliza Doolittle in *My Fair Lady.*

THE FLOWER ROUTE

Flower markets—devoted solely to the sale of flowers—are justifiably popular and much visited. And yet, without wanting to over-generalize, they often suffer from a kind of facile seductiveness and showiness that favors quantity over quality. Europeans are therefore also advised to frequent their large weekly street markets, where a flower stall is always tucked away between, say, a diary stand and the butcher's display. Such stalls are well stocked, sometimes remarkably so, featuring rare or unusual items. At the market on Place d'Aligre in Paris, for example, every June a nice little old lady brings some of her precious treasures to sell. Her display is as modest and unflattering as possible—a few dozen bouquets dumped on newsprint. But what bouquets! Real garden roses, wonderfully leafy and plump, remarkably fragrant. Another stall, at the market on Cours de Vincennes, is easy to miss if shoppers pass too quickly.

And yet in summer it is full of daisies, snapdragons, and cornflowers—an entire range of rural flowers sold directly by a small grower in Noisy-le-Grand, just outside Paris. He is one of the few producers who still bring flowers to market themselves. The merchants behind most stalls are now florists like any others, especially since some of them have recently begun to sell pretty, and even highly refined, arrangements.

Flowers picked up at a street market are still generally bought in bunches, however, constituting the raw material that buyers arrange and compose to their own taste. The street-market ethic still applies—buyers compare, select, and evaluate the freshness of the produce on offer. A first glance is not always sufficient, any more than it is with vegetables: a rosebud will keep its promise only if it is good and firm when pressed gently between thumb and index finger. Similarly, tightly bound stems sometimes mask yellowing leaves that could foretell a premature death. A closer look is called for. Indeed, the flower trade is characterized by artful camouflage as damaging as it is chronic. The origin of the product, for instance, is never marked. Whereas all other market produce is carefully labeled—"juicy oranges from Tunisia," or "green beans from Cameroon"—flowers remain silent. Nor is there much hope of learning more if a vendor is not favorably disposed. Yet the origin of flowers is crucially important, since it gives an idea of the distance they have traveled and the date they were picked. It also provides clues to the personality of a given variety. There is as much difference between a rose from Ecuador and a rose from France as there is between a big firm tomato from Holland and a small ripe one from Italy.

It has now been more than twenty years since the flower trade went global. The phenomenon spurred a sudden, international infatuation with bouquets. The effect was particularly noticeable in the 1980s when there was a striking increase in

Flower stalls in Europe's weekly street markets represent the most traditional form of the flower trade, having hardly changed since the nineteenth century. The quality and variety of flowers and greenery have nevertheless evolved. Not so long ago, it was said that street-market florists made their wholesale purchases at the end of the morning, when only inferior produce was left. Today, however, some of these merchants are as well stocked as established flower shops, offering interesting foliage such as grasses and boughs of blackthorn or black horehound, as well as sophisticated blooms such as fine roses, beautiful hydrangea, and a variety of celosia known as cockscomb (*above*).

both supply and demand, leading to annual growth rates of roughly ten per cent. Since that time, flowers have continued to travel in ever greater numbers on a daily basis, making a global odyssey along highly established routes. Just as traders once followed a Silk Route and a Spice Route, today there exists a veritable Flower Route.

Every day, countless shipments of flowers leave the endless summer of the southern hemisphere to head north. They follow a one-way road, since the flower trade is divided into two distinct worlds. Northern countries consume far more than they produce, and constantly import the rest. Southern regions, in contrast, export almost everything they grow, because no local market exists.

There are, of course, exceptions to this rule: Mexicans, enamored of gladioli, buy 90 per cent of local production, while Argentineans, also "very into glads," absorb it all. It is nevertheless true that many countries that have recently begun floriculture, notably some in Africa, have no floral tradition of their own.

Back in the early 1970s, no one would have predicted this development. The northern hemisphere kept the flower business in the family. The United States, for instance, grew enough to satisfy national demand, which meant a lot of roses and plenty of carnations and chrysanthemums. No surprises here—these three classics constitute the mainstay of the floral trade throughout the world.

California, with its exceptional sunlight and cool Pacific breezes, became a veritable nursery, growing over half the flowers produced in the United States. In sheltered valleys along the coast, fields of flowers stretch as far as the eye can see. Sonoma Valley boasts not only vineyards but also rose gardens full of fine English varieties like "Abraham Darby" with its peony-shaped bloom and superb fragrance. Florida, meanwhile, also has a magnificent climate, enabling it to grow flowers all year long. In Colorado, flowers are grown under clear skies at high altitude. In Pennsylvania and New York, seasonal waves of cold and heat are combatted by age-old techniques brought over by the earliest Dutch settlers. When it comes to exotic flowers, Hawaii provides flaming bushes of anthuriums and splendid bunches of orchids espaliered at the foot of volcanoes.

In short, from New York to Polynesia, there boasts a fine, perhaps unique, range of potential varieties. Yet it no longer suffices. In 1993, the U.S. produced a billion cut flowers, all of which were snapped up. Many more had to be imported, namely 1.6 billion carnations, 260 million chrysanthemums, and 500 million roses in 1993 alone, all air-freighted from Colombia via Miami, the country's major import and distribution hub.

Of all the South American exporters, Colombia has had the most remarkable career. A few crates of flowers were being exported back in 1965, rising modestly in the late 1960s. Today Colombia's

Every August, Medellin hosts the Silleteros Festival, one of the biggest markets in Colombia. This tradition originated when growers in neighboring villages began hauling their flowers to market in a chair (*silla*) strapped to their backs. Since 1957, the flower bearers have organized a big parade which culminates in prizes for the most spectacular and best decorated chairs (*silletas*). The event is as athletic as it is artistic, because the weight of the flowers can be enormous—the 1996 winner of the most monumental chair carried a weight of 120 kg (165 lbs) for over a mile! *Above:* A porter bent under a chair of flowers.

floral revenue amounts to several hundred million dollars per year. It feeds the vast appetite of the American market, now one of the world's largest importers of cut flowers.

Colombia owes its success primarily to large carnations, yet also to miniature, candy-colored varieties—cherry red, sugar white, candy pink. It also exports roses and pompon chrysanthemums. The country's mild, sunny climate (the equal of any greenhouse in the world) and plentiful cheap labor enable Colombians to produce flowers at unbeatable prices. New York and Californian floriculturists, obviously, are less than delighted. Five times in the past decade, Colombia has been

sanctioned for dumping practices, paying heavy duties for selling flowers at less than American production costs.

After a moment of panic—in Bogota, certain producers began pulling up their plants—the Colombians turned to Europe, a continent hungry for bouquet-filling items, especially in winter. Once again, the market took off, especially after 1993 when the European Union abolished tariffs on flowers imported from Andean regions in an effort to encourage coca producers to change crops. The war on drugs thereby elevated Colombia to the rank of the world's second largest exporter of flowers, behind the uncontested

A field of anthurium in a small village in Colombia's Sierra Nevada de Santa Marta, not far from the Caribbean Sea. Most flowers produced in Colombia originate from Western plants. That is why those varieties, especially roses, thrive best on Bogota's temperate "savannah." The climate of this high plateau is pleasant throughout the year, with daytime temperatures ranging from 14° to 20° C (58° to 68° F), cooling to a nightly 4° to 8° C (41° to 47° F). Colombia also cultivates local species such as anthurium, which grows wild in the country's tropical forests and is now highly appreciated as a cut flower.

leader, Holland. Other South American countries took advantage of the tariff break and entered the European market. Ecuador, for instance, has had spectacular success, if more modest than Colombia's. Ecuadorean roses are seen at European florists as soon as the first frosts hit, making local varieties rarer and more expensive.

Strangely, varieties such as "Maya," "Nicole," and "First Red" express a distinctly different charm depending on whether they have been grown in a greenhouse in Provence or under the Ecuadorean sun. They seem to benefit wonderfully from the Andean climate—perhaps a little too much, some people claim.

The enormous buds of roses from Ecuador sit high on a robust stem, displaying all the allure of a fine specimen. What they gain in solidity, they may lose in charm.

Africans have also arrived on the floral scene, turning roses for the European market into one of the continent's new specialties. Only two or three countries have followed a different path: Zimbabwe, for instance, opted for the feathery protea, highly appreciated in cool, dry bouquets; Cameroon and the Ivory Coast, meanwhile, specialize in tropical flowers and greenery. Everywhere else—Tanzania, Zambia, and especially Kenya—the rose continues its heady climb.

Floral customs in Colombia have evolved from local habits, mostly inherited from very old Hispanic traditions. Floral arrangements for celebrations and funerals almost exactly recall the sometimes gigantic mosaics of flowers described in southern Europe in the seventeenth century. *Above:* A small flower merchant at the entrance to Bogota's central cemetery; the florist offers both large funeral compositions (*cascadas*) and ordinary bouquets. Locals often buy their everyday flowers at the cemetery, where prices are much cheaper than at a florist's. *Left:* An arrangement of roses and ferns by Don Eloy Rosas, one of Bogota's leading florists.

The Mediterranean shores have also long supplied Europe. Northern markets still bear the scent of flowers from Israel and Morocco (whose roses have nevertheless been hit by Ecuadorean competition). The grand south–north axis is not the only route taken by flowers, however. Some of them now follow ancient caravan routes straight from the East (airborne, this time, not overland!). Thailand, in particular, ships great quantities of orchids to France.

The Asian continent is nevertheless generally parsimonious with its cut flowers. Nothing arrives from China, nor from Japan. Japan's own production barely meets local needs, for the Japanese not only generate substantial demand but also have very fixed ideas about floral beauty. Alstroemeria, for instance, had to be corrected and modified to meet Japanese aesthetic criteria—the arrangement of the flower's petals was highly appreciated, but not their streaks and stripes.

Plain blooms are so valued in Tokyo that hybrid specialist Isamu Miyake developed a made-to-measure alstroemeria completely free of stripes, requiring fourteen years of research and vast investment. Japan, however, will usually pay whatever it costs.

That, moreover, is the reason the Japanese market is so coveted today, even though few countries have managed to crack it. The Japanese have incredible phytosanitary requirements, and do not really trust anyone except the Dutch. And even then, not completely!

AALSMEER: A MANDATORY STOP ON THE FLOWER ROUTE

Every month, a venerable "quality master" leaves Tokyo for the flower auction at Aalsmeer in Holland. He goes not to buy but to monitor products which will be sent—perhaps—to Japan. No other customer, allegedly, is so wary. Furthermore, to prevent establishing relations that might lead to corruption, the quality master is rotated every three months. Aalsmeer, at any rate, is no joking matter—people there engage in a nerve-wracking business, constantly on the lookout for the arrival of flowers from every continent as cargo planes land at Amsterdam airport. The days are long gone when a few local growers from this little part of Holland got together to manage the sale of their bulbs. They now number five thousand, but they still control operations insofar as the Aalsmeer *bloemenveiling* continues to function as a cooperative. The smokey café where they once gathered was replaced in 1972 by an immense complex which is still the largest flower market on Earth—over 1,800 acres of sheds, the equivalent of 150 soccer fields! Most flowers pass through Aalsmeer, whether headed for London, Berlin, Paris, Rome, or even Hong Kong. It matters little whether they were grown in Colombia, Africa, Israel, or Dutch greenhouses, Aalsmeer is a mandatory stage on the route. The Dutch—who are not only the leading European producer but also the world's leading importer—receive, monitor, and re-export practically

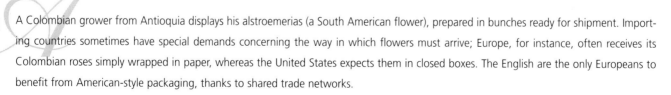

A Colombian grower from Antioquia displays his alstroemerias (a South American flower), prepared in bunches ready for shipment. Importing countries sometimes have special demands concerning the way in which flowers must arrive; Europe, for instance, often receives its Colombian roses simply wrapped in paper, whereas the United States expects them in closed boxes. The English are the only Europeans to benefit from American-style packaging, thanks to shared trade networks.

everything that flowers on the planet. Not content to organize the route, they also set the prices. Wherever a bouquet is bought, even deep in the countryside, its price was probably set that morning, at dawn, in one of Aalsmeer's five action halls.

Business begins at 6:30 a.m. sharp. It requires a clear head: the Dutch auction system demands a good deal of concentration. It takes place in a stepped theater—from which the public is prohibited—opposite large lighted dials under the control of an auctioneer. Each buyer (wholesaler, exporter, or agent) takes a seat behind a numbered desk. Once the session opens, an interminable parade of carts passes by in successive lots of tulips, snowballs, hyacinths, and freesias, so that the merchandise can be assessed at a glance. Meanwhile,

relevant information is posted on the board—name of producer, variety, total quantity available, minimum purchase quantity. Every time the lot changes, the board flashes and the bidding opens again. The most important detail is the little red light that moves around the dial, marked from 100 to 1, indicating a steady decrease in auction price. At any given moment, a buyer can stop the countdown and acquire the lot simply by pressing the button on his or her desk. But if the button is pressed too soon, the buyer will have paid too much for thousands and thousands of flowers; and if the button is pressed a fraction of a second too late, another wholesaler will have already snapped up the lot. Mistakes are costly, at least in principle (magnanimous auctioneers, admitting that a button

The Dutch demonstrated their genius not only in growing flowers but also in organizing the world's trade route for cut flowers. Transportation of these highly perishable goods is a race against the clock. At the Aalsmeer auction halls, flowers have barely been sold before they are already on the way to their destination, placed in buckets of cool water loaded on to carts that automatically take them to their departure point. The incessant parade of tiny trains of flowers through the gigantic halls is immediately followed by a ballet of trucks and cargo planes. Such organization is the fruit of long experience—as early as the 1930s, Aalsmeer flowers were already taking to the air (*above*).

sometimes gets pushed unwittingly, recognize what they call "the right to take a little nap"). When the mistake is so flagrant that laughter breaks out in the hall, the sale is cancelled and the bidding begins again: dials flash, carts pass by, the little red light begins its countdown, a button gets pushed, and the deal is closed. The central computer takes care of the rest. For at that very moment, somewhere else in the vast complex, a printer is already spitting out an invoice for the buyer. Fur-thermore, the buyer's account has already been debited! Credit is not part of the game at Aalsmeer. The motto on every-one's lips is: "Purchased today, paid for today."

No one contests this golden rule, especially since the *bloe-menveiling* respects its part of the contract every day by monitoring a second golden rule: a flower picked one day must be auctioned the next day and delivered that night to anywhere in Europe (or even farther away). That makes a maximum of three days from greenhouse to florist's window. Given that a household bouquet should last for roughly a week, and that, once cut, a flower can survive for ten days, everything adds up. The system seems to work perfectly, at least when the flowers come directly from suppliers in Holland or nearby countries. When it comes to more distant origins, a flower will not reach the florist until the fourth day—at best. At worst, it will have taken much longer. It is not always easy to assess the day of cutting, incidents en route, and more or less long stays in refrigerators. Kept at a temperature of 3° or 4° C (38° F), a flower

goes into suspended animation and, according to certain people, can survive nearly a month. The re-awakening may be tricky, however. When one of these sleeping beauties arrives on market stalls, its frigid face-lift may still fool people. The end is nevertheless near—as soon as it is plunged into a warm apartment, it succumbs to exhaustion. On the eve of major flower-giving holidays such as Valentine's Day and Mother's Day, unscrupulous European growers have been known to employ this type of artifice. Highly coveted vari-eties mysteriously vanish from the market for a week or two prior to the event—hidden in a cold, dark chamber—only to resurface miraculously on D-Day. At a price, of course.

Everyone knows that flowers stay fresh for just a few days or even hours. So Aalsmeer is a constant race against the clock. The carts go straight from the auction chamber to other halls to be prepared for the next stage of the trip. By noon the bidding is over, the sheds are practi-cally empty, and cargo planes, laden with pallets of flowers, are already throttling their engines on the runways. Hundreds of trucks are also warm-ing up, ready to roll once the last crate is loaded. They will fan out across Europe, occasionally dri-ving all night to arrive before city markets open. Some retail florists even receive direct deliveries, several times per week. In certain provincial towns where no wholesale market exists, Dutch truck drivers are greeted like saviors—sometimes a driver is even given the keys to the shop when no one is there at the break of day to take delivery

The traditional image of Holland includes fields of tulips brightening the landscape as far as the eye can see (*right*). Those vast stretches of color are not destined for bouquets, however—they are grown solely for bulb reproduction. Tulips grown for cut flowers are harvested long before they bloom, while buds are still tightly closed. They should just be starting to open when they appear in shop displays like that of Amsterdam florist Thera de Groot (*above*).

of the merchandise. This ability to get on with the job has earned these solo navigators the affectionate nickname of The Flying Dutchmen.

The Dutch thus rule as absolute masters over this sea of flowers. But for how long? The winds seem to be changing. Dutch omnipotence is being imperceptibly weakened by the emergence of new producer countries. And it was the Dutch themselves who created this competition. With their own hands they planted the first Andean and African flowers, anticipating healthy pickings that would further strengthen the Dutch position. Events have overtaken them, however. Africa and Colombia now sometimes skip the Aalsmeer auction. They have their own intermediaries and clients. When Prague and Moscow celebrate Women's Day on 8 March, Bogota now directly dispatches the thousands of red flowers awaited by Eastern European women. These eastern countries are moreover a favorite market for new producers insofar as local floral traditions—which survived through thick and thin—took off again once the Berlin Wall came down. A weakened market position is not the sole effect of the prodigal way in which Holland sowed its skills. It also seeded the planet with an army of identical blossoms encompassing a dozen traditional species at most, from carnations to gerbera. All are impeccable, robust, built for long-haul trips, and calibrated to fit containers—in short, almost perfect. And short on surprise. Putting flowers in uniform is the worst thing that could happen to a bouquet. It means a sure death for all the small producers who continue to grow somewhat capricious flowers that amaze, that demand loving care, and that refuse to blossom when their time has passed. It is precisely these graceful varieties that add charm to the markets of New Covent Garden in London and Rungis in Paris.

The Dutch have always acclimatized exotic flowers, adopting them as their own. Their biggest success was obviously the Levantine tulip. Trade catalogues at Aalsmeer offer forty different varieties of tulip, shipped all over the world. They may be round ("Don Quixote") or slender ("Aladdin") or tousled ("Estella Rijnveld"). In the Singel flower market in Amsterdam (*left*), they blossom in an infinite range of shapes and colors. Anthurium, a much more recent tropical import, does not come in as many varieties. Yet only a few years ago it existed solely in red, whereas it can now be found in white edged with purple, pink flamed with green, and even jade green. *Above:* A bouquet of anthuriums from Gerda's in Amsterdam.

ROWS AND ROWS OF IRISES,
VIOLETS, AND LILAC

From Emile Zola's *Belly of Paris* to Robert Doisneau's photographs, the Paris fruit and vegetable
market known as Les Halles swelled and grew
without ever reorganizing the space attributed to
flowers, already so inconvenient in the nineteenth
century. It was nevertheless there, among picturesque pushing and shoving, that Parisian florists
continued to buy their supplies until the 1960s.
Covent Garden, in London, suffered from the same
problems until 1974 when the flower market,

which had occupied the site for three hundred
years, finally left for Nine Elms. Londoners at least
managed to preserve their magnificent old market
buildings, whereas Baltard's late, lamented pavilions in Paris were demolished. True enough, the old
halls no longer offered the flower trade a future—
vacant spots were impossible to find, and new
arrivals had to be content with a corner of a stall
shared with obliging colleagues. When, on 3 March
1969, the first sale of flowers was held in the new
market of Rungis, outside Paris, everyone finally
had an individual stand. The only notable change,
in fact, was the increased space. Everything else,

Although all European flower markets now dance to Aalsmeer's tune, each has retained its local color. When spring comes to New Covent
Garden, outside London, there is an abundance of simple, typically English garden varieties such as daffodils (the official flower of Wales).
Above: Picturesque negotiations over a bunch of daffodils in the former Covent Garden, 1950. *Right:* The flower market in Paris in the 1950s,
photographed by Robert Doisneau. The opening of a new market in Rungis, outside Paris, has not really changed anything—alleys are still
crowded and stands attractively cluttered.

perhaps out of nostalgia, remained the same—Paris wholesalers brought all their old habits with them, including their stalls, trestle tables, and a kind of gleeful chaos. In short, Rungis is the opposite of Aalsmeer. Some industry professionals regret this, and would willingly swap picturesqueness for improved organization. Visitors do not complain, however. In fact, apart from the particularly unattractive surroundings of Rungis, a trip to the flower market is one of the most pleasant trips imaginable. Just the sight of it is remarkable—and anyway, retail sales to individuals are forbidden. For that matter, New York florists Tom Pritchard and Billy Jarecki, who visited flower markets all over the world for their book, *Mädderlake's Trade Secrets*, fell in love with Rungis: "Here the selection is always varied, sometimes even astounding, but more importantly one finds a pervasive and palpable warmth and joy in the act and art of selling flowers... It was amazing and heartening for us to see that people who have sold vast quantities of flowers every day of their lives can still recognize the beauty and the seductive qualities of their wares." In contrast, certain wholesale markets sell the produce straight out of the boxes in which it arrives.

Dutch influence is detectable in Rungis, as elsewhere. Containers bearing Aalsmeer's stamp—which is basically the only way for international flowers to travel—can be seen everywhere. Yet French flowers, especially those from the south (which dominate until really hot weather hits), ardently defend their turf. Mimosas, violets, ranunculus, ample carnations, and Pro-

vençal tulips (very beautiful and highly sought after) are exported to both Switzerland and the United States. Then there are "Tetra" anemones, the most beautiful of all, which southern producers grow pinkish-white from September to April, then red prior to Christmas, and above all blue for fresh little springtime bouquets. The Dutch, who lack such a pretty variety, regularly order them. Producing flowerets is a tricky art, requiring expert skills that the Riviera shares with Italy (also present at Rungis, even though Germany is a better outlet than France for Italian flowers).

Most of the rows at Rungis are taken up with varieties sent from Holland and the south of France. Florists stroll down these alleys at dawn, doing the rounds of their usual suppliers and picking up along the way whatever they may have reserved on arrival. A florist's talent is evident not only in the way he or she composes bouquets, but also in the way flowers are selected, a personal and difficult task that is never delegated to anyone else. A particularly fine shipment—say, an exceptional color—will not last long on the stands; it has to be spotted before competitors get to it.

Most inventive florists see purchasing as a daily treasure hunt which inevitably leads them down the four most picturesque rows in Rungis, namely violet, lilac, tulip, and iris alleys. That is where "Paris" produce is found, that is to say flowers carefully nurtured in the Paris area. Wholesalers and agents give way here to growers who bring what they have picked that very day (or, at most, the day before). Everything is

As soon as it is cut, a flower's life is endangered. The tiny vessels in its stem may become blocked in a matter of minutes, preventing it from drinking water. That is why growers, when cutting, immediately place flowers in a bucket of cool water mixed with fungicides. Fragile varieties such as sweet peas (*above*) remain in water all the way to the point of sale. Other species, such as violets, are simply sold in boxes— they need merely to be sprinkled with water, since they drink not from their stems but from their corollas. The same thing holds for gerberas, which also travel in dry boxes. *Left:* A stand of gerberas at Rungis.

fresh, unusual, scented, and varied like real garden pickings. The show, alas, is temporary. Paris flowers, which are "real" flowers, bloom only in season. From 20 November onward, there is not a single blossom to be seen on the stands, which anyway are hidden behind a forest of Christmas trees. Those trees, of course, enable growers to get through the early winter months, before deserting the market entirely until the following spring.

The future for these little growers is not bright. Yet giving up "Paris" flowers would represent, in a way, the end of the world for Parisian florists. They are the sole produce likely to provide them with that chiseled, "hand-tooled" flower with a

unique color and just the right degree of bloom. The surviving growers are accustomed to supplying outstanding items, as they have for generations at family firms like Brossard & Fils. Brossard senior originally amazed Paris by secretly developing pompon daisies, soft and round like marshmallow, that made his company's name. The Brossards have been innovating ever since. They cultivate a remarkable, fiery red-and-yellow cockscomb, for example, which glows like coral in the murky light of their greenhouses at Ollainville. Responding to the fashion for green flowers, Brossard even developed a pale jade variety after five years of patient cross-breeding. Such work is always a gamble, since it is impossible to predict the success of a color or how long it will remain in fashion. Things are easier when it comes to sweet peas, another Brossard specialty which has been shipped as far away as Hong Kong. No guesswork is necessary here—as soon as the sweet peas flower, Brossard bypasses nature and endows them with the colors florists demand, namely yellow and orange. He simply gives them a long drink of a saffron-colored liquid he concocted himself. In just a few hours, pink sweet peas become a pretty salmon color, while white ones turn yellow. Nothing too difficult, in short—even the cutting can be done to order, when the petals are just right.

Huge bunches of these patiently worked and prepared flowers hit the road at 5:30 a.m. At the same time, rose dealers are also heading for Rungis. Madame Coquelin, for example, sells the roses her husband cultivates—thirty-five varieties, ten of them fragrant. They are grown just half an hour outside Paris, on a small estate in Mandres-les-Roses. Once again, the quest for novelty is a constant obsession with the Coquelins, who have to keep abreast of fashion. Their greenhouses are constantly evolving—although a rosebush is

The range of natural colors of sweet pea (*above*), as grown by the Brossard firm near Paris. Yellow and orange can be added to this palette by giving the flowers a tinted elixir to drink. The same technique could be used to turn sweet peas blue, but Monsieur Brossard refuses to do so because the color does not spread evenly across the bloom. In the realm of flowers, blue is the rarest and therefore most coveted color. Researchers therefore regularly announce the imminence of that wonder of wonders, a blue rose—which never arrives. Only a few species are naturally blue, such as the delphiniums (*right*) photographed in the Brossard greenhouse.

productive for eight or ten years, the Coquelins regularly uproot and replant. Under a high nave of glass, roses ready to be harvested stretch toward the light in a forest of long, straight stems bearing a single bud. They are cut as soon as the first frill of petal can be seen, which ten years ago would have been considered a rather late harvest. At that time, shops presented bunches of completely closed roses, but nobody wants them today.

It is precisely new tastes and attitudes that Madame Coquelin keeps in mind as she moves up and down her greenhouses. She is particularly satisfied with her "Maya," pearly white edged with pink, a current bestseller which should remain so for a good while yet. The chocolatey "Leonidas" is also popular, as is "Nicole" with its purplish edges. Madame Coquelin is well pleased to have reintroduced the little "Tango," so popular twenty years ago. Also doing well are "Papa Meilland," "Pierre de Ronsard," and "Felicia," which are allowed to flower freely—all three fragrant varieties are

selling increasingly well. The same goes for her green roses (yes, even rose growers had to bend to fashion), which continue to surprise and intrigue people. Madame Coquelin pauses, however, when she comes to the rows of "Kaina"—its fuchsia color has not had much success, even though in small quantities it makes a fine effect in a bouquet. The fate of "Mascara," "Pavarotti," and "Ravel" is already sealed. All are too insipid and old-fashioned, and will be ripped out next year. Florist Christian Tortu refuses to take any more of

them, and regularly asks Madame Coquelin when she plans to dump her "Barbie roses"! Replacements will therefore have to be found. With a little luck and a lot of intuition, Madame Coquelin's choices will answer the prayers of florists at her stand in Rungis.

In fact, the search for small, conscientious, and imaginative growers has become a key concern for good florists in all Western countries. In Covent Garden, too, Dutch flowers coexist alongside local, typically English varieties—cornflowers, peonies, Guernsey roses, and Lincolnshire daffodils. Until recently, only a handful of florists were interested in this local production. Customers, who rarely bother to vary their bouquets, never asked for them.

Yet such flowers are now being rediscovered, even as far away as the United States. Such is the moving story of the Garibaldi family, which has been growing violets on green slopes south of San Francisco for four generations. It was nearly one hundred years ago that grandfather Garibaldi, an Italian immigrant, began growing the "Blue Giant." His descendants followed through thick and thin, even when violets met with total indifference. By 1980, all other producers were ripping out their plants. That was when Floreal, the San Francisco florist, asked the Garibaldis to supply them with violets for tiny wreaths and for graceful bouquets with silk ribbons. Ever since, customers—who had forgotten what violets smell like—have been expressing amazement that such pretty little things are still being grown.

Roses grown in the Paris region are internationally renowned. A visit to the greenhouses where they are grown, however, reveals little of their future splendor, since the rosebushes are never allowed to blossom. Although roses are now picked later than was once the case, they are cut as soon as the bud shows a little slip of color—the first wave of petals. Only imperfect or unfashionable roses are permitted to bloom. *Above:* In an abandoned greenhouse in Brie, an outmoded rose unfolds its petals for the last time. *Left:* A display of roses (*top*) in the boutique of Didier-Pierre, who supplies the Paris region during the flowering season; Didier-Pierre also has "Léonidas" roses (*bottom*), known for their chocolatey color.

Masters
of Floral Art

It has become extremely fashionable during the past decade or so to have a strong opinion on bouquets and floral art (just as, in the eighteenth century, socialites were conversant in botany and, later, in the language of flowers). Today it is chic to frequent the boutique of a trendy florist where all the best people go, including a few leading celebrities. The latest twist is to be a personal friend of the florist, who is now as famous and sought after as the clientele. Fashionable florists have difficulty finding the time to fulfill all their responsibilities, beginning with professional ones, which include dawn visits to flower markets and late nights at the shop making last-minute arrangements for a chic wedding or fashion show. Meanwhile, leading florists are also expected to plane-hop to the four corners of the Earth. Kenneth Turner, from London, may be summoned to Venice to decorate a palatial banquet or to New York to do the Thanksgiving table for a rich American hostess. Some florists travel in order to participate in scholarly symposiums, such as Daniel Ost from Belgium and Gregor Lersche from Germany, both of whom are international celebrities, especially in Japan. Still others export their style, opening branches all over the world, which means keeping an eye on everything. Christian Tortu, for instance, shuttles at a hellish pace between his boutiques in Paris, New York's Fifth Avenue, Singapore, and Jakarta. It might be

added that these masters of an ephemeral art have also become theorists, taking up the pen in the same way that great chefs now do. Florists write how-to books that include some of their "recipes," poetic volumes in which they wax philosophical, and lavish art books which present flowers as sculpture—there are now enough titles to establish a library devoted exclusively to flowers! Germans and Anglo-Americans are quite prolific in this sphere: all their famous florists have published at least one book. The same is not yet true in France, but soon will be.

Thirty years ago, florists were simple shopkeepers. Today they are media stars. If, in addition to floral talent, they are articulate, the press will adore them. And if, furthermore, a florist is handsome, so much the better. "Handsome" is used advisedly here, because the floral trade has now become predominantly masculine.

There are exceptions to this rule—in 1997, three of the five florists honored with the title of Finest Artisans of France were women, while in England, Paula Pryke and Jane Packer, among others, are very fashionable. A masculine perspective on flowers is nevertheless one of the indisputable characteristics of the modern era. Is it this male sensibility, then, that led to the popularity and vitality of a new, freer, bolder floral art? Not necessarily—the way was paved long ago by a woman, namely Constance Spry.

Leading florists now have international reputations. Kenneth Turner, from England, decorates palaces the world over. *Above:* Kenneth Turner and his team decorate one of his London shops. The Dane Erik Bering, florist to the queen of Denmark, designs the weddings for Western aristocracy. Another Dane, Tage Andersen, who has been in the forefront of the European flower scene for the past thirty years, is respected well beyond Copenhagen. *Left:* Tage Andersen in his boutique. Floral art no longer has any borders or limits—Dutchman Marcel Wolterinck considers it a question of total lifestyle to the extent of releasing a compact disc to which he orchestrates his floral designs. *Previous pages:* Festoons of roses by Erik Bering (*left*), and a "Black Magic" rose in a pewter vase (*right*) by Marcel Wolterinck.

CONSTANCE SPRY:
INVENTING MODERN BOUQUETS

Although little known in France, Constance Spry is venerated in England, where she was one of the greatest florists of the 1930s. She came to flowers somewhat by chance, with no particular training. She just happened to like flowers, not as a professional but as a homemaker. Indeed, her genius resided in exploiting the simplicity of domestic bouquets, composed casually of whatever is available with one hand even as the other hand is plumping cushions on the sofa or straightening the curtains. In short, she put life back into bouquets. This went completely against the grain of what was fashionable in England at the time. On the eve of the First World War, florists were still cultivating hothouse flowers, tight bouquets, and Victorian posies. Spry, however, preferred unpretentious flowers, wild grasses, and tousled roses, all woven into unpredictable, curvaceous, deliberately asymmetrical arrangements. She delighted her friends with these pretty extravagances, bedecking their apartments and parties with flowers all the more freely insofar as she did it privately for a number of years.

Spry opened her first London shop, Flower Decorations, only in 1928. She immediately won public attention with her decoration of the windows of Atkinsons perfumery on Old Bond Street. Her spectacular display was unlike anything seen at the time: she combined large branches of foliage with wild and cultivated flowers, placing bouquets in soapstone urns and black marble bowls held aloft by wooden angels. The windows became so famous that Flower Decorations was soon drawing many of London's leading figures, such as the Prince of Wales and Mrs Simpson. Syrie Maugham, wife of Somerset Maugham and a fashionable decorator in her own right, was even won over to Spry's penchant for "white on white." Armfuls of white flowers arranged in a totally white apartment remained the height of elegance for two decades.

Spry's art, in fact, was not limited to composing bouquets, but espoused a global view, stressing the character of the room in which flowers were displayed. The insistence on seeing a flower blossom in just the right setting was a veritable innovation, and remains one of the golden rules of floral decoration today. This quest for harmony also meant that the choice of vase became crucial, to such an extent that Spry began designing her own models. She had a predilection for Medici vases—a stone urn with flared bowl—but did not hesitate to use a range of diverse items from tea cups to shells via bamboo shafts. Today's florists play endlessly on the original use of various objects, some of them far removed from the standard idea of a vase, and people are no longer very startled. Yet when Spry introduced the concept, it was remarkably bold. Similarly, her centerpieces were also surprising at the time—red peppers and a scattering of beans or roses blanketing the foot of a large spray of laurel, flowering

The duke and duchess of Windsor were among the most faithful clients of English florist Constance Spry (*above*). She handled the floral decoration of their wedding, which took place in France in 1937. Spry's work, under the circumstances, was particularly appreciated, as witnessed by the duchess's dedication of a photograph taken by Cecil Beaton (*right*). It is touchingly signed "Wallis," the duchess's first name.

Cecil Beaton

To Mrs Spry
who made my
wedding so lovely
Wallis
June 3rd — 1937

mint, rosemary, and Queen Anne's lace. Spry also revealed the beauty of vegetables—a bowl of purple artichokes simply set in their own velvety gray leaves. In short, she invented it all. She also spread her ideas by publishing thirteen books and founding a school, transforming floral art in both Europe and the United States. The transformation did not occur overnight, however. In 1953, when Spry decorated the processional route for Queen Elizabeth's coronation (earning her an OBE), standard florist bouquets were still very strait-laced and rather uninventive.

The 1950s tend to evoke two or three standard recollections of flowers, usually linked to emotional reactions associated with the maternal image. Many American women, for instance, fondly recall that the prettiest flowers in the house were found neither in the living room nor on the dining table, but rather in the refrigerator on Sunday morning. That is where mother, returning from an evening on the town or at the theater, had placed her corsage of gardenias. Those snowy blossoms, frozen in their cellophane setting, enthralled every little girl.

French women tend to remember the famous bunch of red "Baccarat" roses that young fathers lovingly offered their wives. Huge bouquets of gladioli were also an almost mandatory domestic ornament—some women remember being so "stuffed" with them in childhood that it took years to recover. Such bouquets remained neat, clean, and tidy, reflecting the "homemaking" ethic. Housewives with their impeccable permanent hairdos were hallowed at the time, newly freed from household drudgery thanks to modern kitchen appliances. They could devote themselves

In the 1930s, Constance Spry was a leading light of London's artistic intelligentsia. She was a friend of the painter Gluck (1875–1978), whose flower pieces were highly appreciated during the interwar period and clearly reflected the influence of the famous florist. The bouquet of *Lilies* that Gluck painted for the London residence of Lord Vernon (*above*) bears all the hallmarks of Spry's style. The shape of the vase is the one she preferred—a sober bowl in perfect harmony with the elegant simplicity of the arum lilies. Bouquets composed of a single variety of long-stemmed flowers would remain in vogue into the 1950s. A large clutch of gladioli, for instance, was used to set off a ball gown designed by Balmain (*right*), photographed by Cecil Beaton in 1951.

completely to decorating the home, and it became almost a moral duty—as in the nineteenth century—to bring flowers into the house, although there were no longer servants to prepare bouquets and change the water. Courses on flower arranging boomed as women learned for themselves. The 1950s therefore hinted at a new type of demand for flowers, a broader and more democratic one.

The flower trade, however, was not sufficiently organized to respond to that demand. Little existed between the extremes of chic, costly bouquets and ordinary market flowers. At one end were the high temples of floral art—suppliers to stars, heads of state, and royalty. In London this meant the firms of Moyses Stevens (established in 1876) and Edward Goodyear (supplier to the royal household since the days of Queen Victoria). In Paris, Lachaume still held sway, continuing to cultivate unusual orchids and create astounding baskets of flowers in a setting of marble, fountains, and rockeries. Then came a complete vacuum until the level of downmarket florists was reached. And in some provincial towns there were no florists at all!

Parisians at least benefited from an interesting, modern initiative in 1937 when André Baumann founded the Maison des Fleurs (now gone) in the heart of Montparnasse. On rainy days, its forty-foot-long window display cast a rainbow of countless colored reflections on shiny sidewalks. Equally spectacular was the store's attractive staircase up to a gallery that ringed a vast space like the ballroom of some transatlantic liner. The

Maison des Fleurs was one of a kind—open, friendly, with a few armchairs here and there for contemplating the beautiful, blossoming space. Since he stayed open late, Baumann was soon drawing the night crowd from La Coupole, the famous restaurant nearby, and lines of swanky cars began parking up and down the sidewalk. For many years, the Maison des Fleurs was the most popular florist in Paris. Although Baumann ran an elegant shop, he was shrewd enough to realize that the trade needed democratizing. He therefore decided to sell flowers "American-style," which meant just as they came, in cardboard boxes, so that his customers—increasingly female—could arrange them as they wished. Baumann even went one step farther—he put price stickers on his flowers! This practice was unthinkable in the finest firms, but other florists followed suit, drawing customers who had never dared to enter chic stores. Furthermore, Baumann dispatched bouquets whenever and wherever desired, both in France and abroad.

The 1950s was also a great period for sending flowers more or less everywhere around the world, thanks to the spread of the system of having one florist transmit an order to another florist at the point of destination. It was back in 1946 that European and American florists jointly founded Interflora, a worldwide organization based on the FTD (Florist Telegraph Delivery Association) which maintained an absolute monopoly on long-distance flowers up to the early 1990s, especially in North America. "Say it with flowers," had become an international slogan.

After the Second World War, flowers were more than ever a key accessory of feminine elegance. Starlets at the Cannes Film Festival were photographed buying flowers (*above*, in 1956), while on the race track at Ascot, young beauties garnished their plunging necklines with roses (*right*). Lauren Bacall, meanwhile, sported an enormous corsage of orchids the day she married Humphrey Bogart (*far right*). Courses and contests in flower arranging were also very popular (*top right*). In Paris, the Lachaume boutique (*top left*) made every floral dream come true—it provided a little desk for customers, where celebrities from all over the world wrote the private messages that were enclosed with the flowers.

FLOWER POWER:
FREE THE BOUQUET

Something was still missing. Flowers were not yet having fun. They were still straightjacketed in wire (because stems had to stand straight), still knotted with ribbon, still wearing a plume of asparagus. What they needed was a jolt of youth. They got this in the 1960s. Fashion model Twiggy was just seventeen when she made the cover of *Vogue* in 1967, sporting a painted flower on her face and wearing a fur coat with a large floral pattern. That same year, the hippy movement spread from the United States to Europe, and countless flowers flooded the West. "Flower power" was above all a bouquet of symbols, a composition based on a return to nature and to innocence, on the power of imagination and love. And on equality of the sexes—garlands of flowers, directly inspired by trips to India, began to adorn long-haired boys as well as girls. Young men could freely appreciate and even wear flowers, which henceforth adopted a masculine face.

This floral revolution swept into flower shops almost effortlessly. Everything went from being glum and conventional to suddenly becoming extraordinary. Some Parisians remember being truly shocked when strolling down Rue de Buci in the 1970s and stumbling upon a florist called La Grange à Buci. People in the know came specially to admire the storefront—not only was it

Florists were not the only people to set floral fashion. Certain celebrities, notably women, also contributed a great deal. Jackie Kennedy, on arriving at the White House, was appalled by the stiffness of bouquets she found there. She immediately abandoned all the varieties conventionally used in presidential offices, and brought in wicker baskets full of garden flowers—anemones, freesias, branches of apple flowers, and of course daisies, which became the flower of the 1960s. *Above:* Jacqueline Kennedy and Madame de Gaulle, each holding a bouquet, during a reception at France's presidential palace in 1961.

exceptional for the time, nothing like it has ever been seen since. Flowers were freeing themselves from convention in those affluent, optimistic days, and La Grange à Buci presented veritable tapestries of flowers, velvety piles of blossoms in astonishing color combinations. It took fifteen florists and seven hours of daily preparation to set up the display!

A total metamorphosis of the trade occurred with incredible spontaneity and gaiety. In France, the new trend remained limited to a small circle, and went almost unperceived by the general public. Things were different, however, in the United States. The press got hold of the phenomenon, and when famous New York florist Ronaldo Maia published his first book in 1978 *The New York Times* praised the originality of his work, which had already been seen in home-decoration magazines.

Maia's book was striking because it conveyed the true fun of working with flowers. Other florists echoed his attitude of "less technique, more fun." Maia simply provided readers with a few basic rules, most of which were based on sound principles established by Constance Spry.

First of all, abandon preconceived ideas: all flowers are worthy, from little, enamel-colored zinnias, cosmos and phlox, to outmoded varieties such as stiff gladioli, which Maia courageously rehabilitated. He cut them very short, gave them some density, bent what remained of the stems, and grouped the flowers in clusters. His gladioli were unrecognizable, and madly charming. Maia

also lauded vegetables, of course, employing a bunch of radishes, a bouquet of tomatoes, and an enormous cauliflower in whose leaves he nested a few pretty rosebuds. When it came to overall harmony, he claimed that every setting called for its own bouquet, every bouquet its own vase. Maia went much further than Spry when it came to vases—wine and liqueur bottles, vegetable crates, cake molds, jam pots, test tubes, and even goldfish bowls (where he consigned flowers like sea-anemones).

Floral art built on these foundations for the next two decades. Much remained to be done even after Maia published his book. The palette of colors was still limited, and bouquets tended to be "all flowers." Maia might include a few boughs of galax (a robust evergreen with shiny leaves), but little other greenery. When it came to streaked, curly, fragrant, wild, or exotic foliage, the time was not yet ripe.

In 1967, French fashion designer Courrèges sowed daisies everywhere (*above* and *lower left*). Every young woman in Paris and London sported this flower, internationally famous for revealing the truth behind a lover's intentions. Yet whereas daisies offer English and Americans a binary option—"He loves me, he loves me not"—the French enjoy several possibilities—"He loves me a little, he loves me a lot, he loves me passionately, he loves me wildly. . . he loves me not." Whatever the case, flowers still offer the shortest route from one heart to another, and by the early 1970s the long-distance delivery service was booming. Interflora was known for its particularly inventive advertising campaigns (*top*).

FLOWER FASHION
OR FASHION FLOWERS

The minor revolution in fresh flowers also affected the parallel realm of silk flowers. As the 1970s dawned, the artificial flower trade underwent a major transformation. Traditionally associated with hat-making, this very Parisian craft was hit hard by the steady decline of hats. Prior to 1930, every woman required at least three hats during the year: a flowered straw hat for Easter, something a little more sober for All Saints' Day in November, and another mid-season hat with feathers and flowers for special occasions and outings. There was enough business to keep several workshops going until everyone went around bare-headed. A few specialized firms nevertheless continued to make artificial bouquets for interiors, and sprigs of silk flowers that some confectioners and chocolatiers put on their boxes. In 1970, alas, a tidal wave hit Paris in the form of silk flowers "made in Hong Kong"—less sophisticated than the Paris originals, of course, but one-tenth the cost! In short, the 277 flower and feather workshops that existed in Paris in 1946 have been reduced to only three today: Lemarié (founded in 1880 by a feather-worker herself), Légeron (founded the same year, originally specializing in leaves and pistils), and Guillet (which celebrated its 100th anniversary in 1996). These three master workshops ingeniously invented a new image for their flowers, rejuvenating the trade.

Just when "real" florists were beginning to enhance their bouquets with everything they could find in greenhouses and country fields, these expert flower-makers were exploring their own backyard. They discovered fabulous collections of punches and dies, some of them very ancient, for cutting multiple shapes from poplin, organza, and velvet, mimicking every petal under the sun, from the large trumpet of arum lilies to the complex butterfly wings of wisteria via honeysuckle buds and daisy skirts. Shelves and shelves of these tools are stored in the Lemarié and Légeron ateliers, carefully labeled with the name of the flower, like a herbal. At the Guillet firm, metallic blooms are stacked from floor to ceiling, rising into the attic. Then there are waffling irons and other precious tools that breathe the illusion of life into leaves, differentiating the fine ribbing of hazel leaves from ivy, strawberry, and even water-lily leaves. This priceless hoard of shapes and patterns has been assembled over the years through purchase and inheritance, and piously preserved. They are all irreplaceable—should a punch get lost or break, a flower will vanish for ever. In recent years, artisans have played on this metallic gene pool, crossing floral traits like true horticulturists and inventing nature anew. This task requires enthusiasm and determination. Everything else comes down to old-fashioned trade secrets. Colorists, for instance, know just how to recreate the subtle shade of a rose by dipping small wads of petals in solutions carefully dosed with pigment. Each firm has

With the exception of daisies, flowers did not play much of a role in fashion design in the 1960s and 1970s. They were too closely associated with hats, which had gone completely out of fashion (*above*, c. 1950). They also corresponded to a conventional, outmoded image of womanhood. Once this crisis passed, silk flowers began making a comeback in new colors and new forms. *Right:* Around 1993, gold- and champagne-colored flowers became fashionable at weddings, as reflected in this bridal gown of Calais lace and pleated tulle by Jean-Paul Mattera, with flowers produced by the Légeron workshop.

its "house recipe," differing from one workshop to another. Other secrets are physical—each petal is worked by hand with a hot iron (plus an arsenal of balls and tweezers) to curl, goffer, flute, puff, or round it. Only then may petals be assembled into a blossom, and set on a stem. A few square inches of muslin or percale is thus suddenly transformed into a blossoming ranunculus or a fleshy orchid. The effect is magical, and always original—a million miles from Hong Kong's artificial flowers. The difference, of course, comes from beauty and imagination, both of which are priceless.

Major fashion designers immediately grasped this language. Haute couture, for that matter, has never really given up flowers. Even straight skirts of the 1960s played at "she loves me, she loves not." Leading designers, moreover, look upon flowers as a good-luck charm. Christian Dior, for example, has a fetish for lily-of-the-valley. When the famous Dior firm celebrated its fiftieth anniversary in 1997 at the Metropolitan Museum of Art in New York, the banquet tables were dressed in organdy tablecloths embroidered with lily-of-the-valley, and ten thousand sprigs of the fragrant little bells adorned the tables. Balmain, meanwhile, has always had a soft spot for violets, whereas Yves Saint-Laurent's elective affinities run toward "Casablanca" lilies and more especially roses (inspiring his perfume called "Paris"). Coco Chanel, of course, preferred the scent of jasmine, as immortalized in No. 5, but ultimately chose the unscented camellia as her emblem.

Chanel's camellias are the great specialty of Monsieur Lemarié. His firm has not always made flowers, having started with feathers. Traditionally, of course, a feather-maker's aigrettes, plumes, and down were used in fancy artificial bouquets. That spurred Lemarié to buy up several interesting collections of punches and embossing dies in 1970, and to begin making flowers for the fashion trade. These days, as real gardens bloom with *japonica* and *reticulata* camellias, Lemarié is busy cultivating countless varieties of the *chanel* species—camellias of black silk muslin, camellias in thermoplastic Rhodoid (impeccable and very chic), and even camellias in gold leaf.

Monsieur Légeron followed the same path, abandoning decorative bouquets at about the same time (once Asian flowers tarnished their image) in order of focus on haute couture. His workshop on Rue des Petits-Champs has the charm of an old-fashioned haberdashery with long wooden counters and stacks of boxes. Everything overflows—muslin garlands cascade on to multicolored blossoms wrapped in tissue paper, ready to adorn the cream of Paris society. Légeron's flowers are set on ready-to-wear hats, hair combs, and chokers, or sewn on to dazzling haute couture evening gowns.

The story is different with Marcelle Lubrano-Guillet, granddaughter of the founder of Guillet, which specializes in interior decoration. Her penchant for inventiveness, profusion, and even mad extravagance has enabled the workshop to survive the industry shake-out.

The petals of these roses (*above* and *right*) made for Dior by Légeron are silk, the leaves velvet. Producing this type of flower is complex, because each rose is composed of dozens of petals of varying size and shape, and the color must be modulated from the outer edge to the center. As for the leaves, several types of fabric punch are required.

In the past two generations, Guillet has decorated absolutely everything in flowers—glamorous chateaus, gatherings at the Paris opera house, ballets given by the marquis de Cuevas, and the Aga Khan's residences. Then there were window displays for Guerlain, Lancôme, and Cartier, plus nine thousand black-eyed Susans for Vuitton, three thousand irises for the Galeries Lafayette department store, and five thousand silk roses to dress the little Eve designed by Jean-Paul Goude for the launching of Cacharel's new scent, Eden. It was a only short step from there to the fashion runways of grand designers, and so Madame Lubrano-Guillet became another "haute couture florist" by supplying Christian Lacroix, Thierry Mugler, Sonia Rykiel, and Louis Féraud.

Everything is done in the finest tradition of elegance and skill, with a new dash of wit and cheekiness. Designer flowers no longer necessarily reflect the discreet charm of the bourgeoisie, as demonstrated by the heaps of flowers insolently garnishing Paris collections during the 1997 spring–summer shows. Dior had recourse to bouquets of organza orchids in "tiger" and "panther" prints, as well as breath-taking exotic flowers; Givenchy's white stretch boots were stitched with blossoms that climbed to the thighs; Gaultier's bride, in addition to her net tights, wore a very classic lily corsage—pinned to the base of her spine, however, as if to say, "Follow me, fella."

Fashion flowers are game for anything, including garish tones and clashing colors. Lubrano-Guillet produced blooms in shocking pinks and purple for London designer Basia Zarzycka. Légeron's daisies for Kenzo were anisette and lemon yellow. Bold color is the major achievement of bouquets—both real and artificial—as the twentieth century draws to a close.

A flowered shoe (*above*) designed by Basia Zarzycka. Color is a crucial ingredient for London designer Zarzycka. The bold colors she chooses for her models are studied and interpreted by Marcelle Lubrano-Guillet of the Guillet flower workshop. Once the dyes have been determined, Guillet's "dipper" has the job of getting the silk to dye correctly—his tricky task involves dipping wads of pre-cut silk in dye mixtures for which only he knows the formula. To get the color just right, petals are sometimes touched up with a brush, one by one.

TRENDS: NEW COLORS, ROSES ONLY

There was a time when florists and customers worried more about the type of flower than its color. A tame 1960s bouquet would be composed of two irises, three gerberas, and an arum lily. As long as it contained some hothouse flowers, a bouquet was considered elegant. Chromatic effect was unimportant (and often unsuccessful). The current trend is just the opposite—today's boutiques, especially in France, display their wares in broad swaths of color. Bouquets, too, now feature blocks of colors and a penchant for strong contrasts. The finicky monochrome effect is completely outmoded. Lively, surprising colors are what work. Green, in particular, has encountered unexpected success recently—although known to add a touch of freshness, green was generally associated with leaves rather than flowers. Now, however, green roses and tulips are as popular as jade anthurium and large arums streaked with emerald. The vogue for immature blooms and early-cut snowballs also provides a touch of acid green as they just begin to flower. Then there are strange inflorescences that retain a leafy color, such as euphorbia and black horehound. Thus the boundary between leaf and flower has almost disappeared, along with the hierarchy dividing them. Florists now sell bunches of greenery, for they appreciate the pastoral charm of horsetail, raspberry, and oak as much as the classic beauty of roses, especially since certain shrubs are delicately scented. Parisian florist Henri Moulié makes a point of gathering lentisk, boxwood, lavender, rosemary, myrtle, and wild thyme from Mediterranean garrigues in order to compose "maquis bouquets" which contain nothing but greenery yet which perfume a room for days on end.

Whereas this enthusiasm for green and greenery would have been considered eccentric a decade ago, the recent popularity of yellow is less surprising. Yellow is a natural color for spring flowers throughout the West, and yellow bouquets have always been in demand as soon as warm weather arrives. Yet it also used to trigger a certain reticence, probably because the language of flowers associated it with infidelity. Since such precaution no longer pertains, the entire range of yellows, from lemon to dark ocher, has become highly popular. Shades of orangey yellow are particularly appreciated, sparkling in pink and green bouquets or bursting into flame against deep purples. Perhaps this color represents a return to the 1970s, as does a resurgence of distinctive flowers like gerbera, which had fallen out of fashion. When the Printemps department store organized its springtime display in 1996, florist Baptiste designed an entire passageway decorated in white and orangey gerbera. In fact, Baptiste rehabilitated outmoded varieties on every floor of the store, notably clusters of arum lilies on Veronese-green plinths and superb arrangements of gladioli in pink, fuchsia, and—obviously—yellow-orange.

Until recently, the color of bouquets was highly codified—tones were carefully "matched" to produce a monochromatic effect. Today, no one worries about clashing colors. Harper & Tom's in London, for instance, does not flinch at the violent encounter of reds, coral, and fuchsia in their display of tulips, roses, and anemones (*above*). Shop displays, for that matter, once based on floral variety, are now organized entirely around color, as seen at Catleya in Brussels (*right, top left*). Today's favored harmonies include yellowed freshened with green, seen again at Catleya (*top right*) and at Atmosphere in Paris (*bottom left*). Finally, the color of the vase can play a crucial, studied role in these tonal compositions, notably at Marianne Robic's boutique in Paris (*bottom right*).

This color revival has greatly benefited roses. Green varieties are appreciated primarily for their strangeness. Warmer tones, meanwhile, have become wonderfully luminous and dazzling, as seen in "Texas," "Ambiance" (a veritable sunset in itself), "Marella" (gilded and fragrant), and the notorious chocolate-brown "Léonidas." These developments have challenged the image of the red rose, and especially the habit of composing monochrome bouquets. Roses are increasingly being arranged in mixed shades. The real novelty, however, which was all the talk of the early 1990s, has been the extreme enthusiasm for roses. An international fever has set in. "Everyone's in love with roses," claims Marlo Phillips, a Manhattan florist who was one of the first to launch the vogue for roses arranged in large balls. "We'll be eating them soon, for all I know!" Some shops now sell nothing but roses. Rosa Rosa in New York, for instance, takes delivery of over eight-hundred dozen roses four times a week, and everything is sold by the end of the afternoon. Some customers phone every day to make sure that their favorite variety has been reserved; others, in greater hurry, send their

limousine over immediately. Another New York firm, Roses Only, has four stores and sells exclusively Ecuadorean roses, usually in full bloom—these days, people buy roses at the peak of their beauty. The same rage hit France in 1991, when Au Nom de la Rose opened its first store and adopted the motto, "Roses, only roses, endless roses." Twelve more shops have subsequently opened, most in Paris but some in the provinces. They sell more that forty varieties, grown in Provence or imported from Ecuador during the winter. Home delivery is provided by liveried pages, who carry anything from a simple bouquet wrapped in white paper to a heart-shaped cushion of roses for lovers.

Hearts of dried roses are also very popular. Dried flowers in general have evolved a great deal and are enjoying a minor revival. Dried bouquets formerly varied little, relying on blue statice and everlasting. They have recently been enhanced with graceful varieties such as peonies and, of course, every kind and color of rose imaginable. More was needed, however—a pledge of undying love requires flowers that seem eternally fresh, which no one had managed to produce. Recently, amazing

Some florists claim to have "invented" round bouquets, others profess to have rediscovered garden roses. Floral fashion, in fact, is often just a new interpretation of old customs. For a bouquet of roses bound in two places (*above*), called a "Brussels bouquet," Dutch florist Marcel Wolterinck employed a traditional technique used by growers in Brussels, who used to bind fragile freesias twice. Similarly, the new passion for roses represents a return to romanticism. *Right:* The table in the apartment that Chopin shared with French novelist George Sand; both were crazy about each other and about roses.

results have been achieved with domestic recipes using glycerin as a preserving agent. The principle behind the idea is simple enough, and was notably developed by Verdissimo, a workshop in Provence. Verdissimo replaces a flower's organic sap with tinted, artificial sap. The exchange occurs almost naturally: the day it is picked, a flower is plunged into an elixir of eternal youth, and is allowed to drink its fill. That is all it takes. Unfortunately, for the moment few varieties of flowers accept this alchemy. Apart from hydrangeas, only roses—thank heavens!—are willing to cooperate. Roses absorb the tinted sap wonderfully: colors stay radiant, blossoms retain their roundness, and petals remain supple and soft to the touch for years! They

inspired Christian Tortu to design fanciful light fixtures, making lamp shades and multibranched lights with silky petals that give interiors an exquisite, flowery glow. Martin Robinson, in London, has devoted himself entirely to these flowers, designing his own vases in terracotta or painted metal, then filling them with short, unpretentious bouquets of "eternal" roses.

Bouquets have continued to evolve toward greater simplicity: shorter stems, smaller volumes. Round bouquets have become popular in the past decade, for they are practical and go in every kind of vase. This trend is nearly universal, although national preferences emerge from one country to another.

"Preserved" roses are one of the most magical developments of recent years. The Verdissimo firm grows roses in Ecuador, where the climate produces robust buds. The preservation process takes place on site, because the technique demands flowers picked that very day if the roses are to enjoy eternal youth. Once they have absorbed a miraculous sap, the roses burst with eternal freshness. They are then sold directly to florists and decorators in the form of petals or whole blooms. The same process can be applied to all kinds of foliage—palm, ivy, asparagus fern, oak, or beech—often used in arrangements of silk or dried flowers.

AMERICAN FLOWERS, OR
FLORAL DESIGNERS

"Will sunflowers still be all the rage this year?" That is the question American florists asked themselves throughout the 1990s. The local sunflower was indeed in vogue, literally bewitching American customers. All kinds of sunflower then invaded European stores. This was no coincidence, for the United States now shapes international trends. The European enthusiasm for lisianthus, another American variety, almost certainly came from America—it was popular across the Atlantic long before Europe began to use it as a cut flower around 1994. Other customs and preferences, on the other hand, do not cross borders. The old world still ignores dogwood, so appreciated in weddings in the southern U.S. for making arches, wreaths, and garlands. And the American habit of using geraniums, begonias, and other flowers generally potted in Europe, is a flight of fancy only occasionally permitted by European florists. Continental florists are also cautious about the multicolored, multifloral bouquets advocated for the past twenty years by the likes of Tom Pritchard and Billy Jarecki of Mädderlake. The American

style can be defined as airy, with no apparent structure, and full of different varieties: a yellow rose, two or three brown roses, a salmon poppy, a branch of apple flowers, scabious, a bunch of fuchsia primrose, and a sprig of love-in-a-mist. The effect is much trickier to achieve than it might appear, and

somewhat resembles seventeenth-century flower paintings. There is a tendency in the United States to perceive flowers bloom by bloom rather than as a dense cluster, which also explains the popularity of centerpieces that juxtapose many small vases, each with a different flower.

Bouquets, however, are not really an American specialty. U.S. florists concentrate on decorating handsome apartments, receptions, and weddings. Passers-by are unlikely to drop into a flower shop for a spontaneous purchase in American cities where, for that matter, people rarely venture out on foot. A sudden urge for a small bouquet will probably be satisfied at the grocery store, which also sells bouquets. Only when it comes to more serious, expensive affairs do Americans turn to florists, who often style themselves "floral designers" and work out of an office. The most famous do not even have a boutique—New York floral celebrities such as Philip Baloun and Robert

In the wake of Constance Spry, English and American floral designers actively helped to change tastes. In the 1970s, for instance, this composition (*above*) by Ronaldo Maia from New York seemed very modern—cutting the gladioli very short was a bold move that rehabilitated a completely outmoded flower. Americans really show their talent, however, when creating overall settings. Designing the flowers for a wedding, for instance, is a subject that fascinates everyone in America and is featured in many publications. *Top:* A wedding chapel decorated with an arch of forsythia and mimosa by Valorie Hart.

Isabell receive clients in their design studio, by appointment only. The same holds for Dorothy Wako, who can be reached only by telephone, and only for a good reason, since she works exclusively for elegant parties, celebrations, and inaugurations at the Museum of Modern Art. Wako's decors are always very elaborate and even scholarly; for the opening of the Picasso–Braque exhibition, she carefully studied the cubist painters' palette before filling basins with "Marella" roses blended with hydrangeas, apricot dahlias, peach-

colored parrot tulips, and a touch of pale blue delphiniums.

Flowers are so closely associated with interior decoration in the U.S. that it is only natural that interior designers dictate colors and fashions. Regional differences in interior decoration therefore govern specific floral styles, a rather strange phenomenon discussed in the January 1997 issue of the trade magazine *Flowers*. In Florida, apparently, living rooms (of linen, sisal, and other fibers) and bedrooms (featuring a large white

A mixture of anemones, pink arums, hyacinths, poppies, and nerine lilies (*above*). The attractive jumble of blooms is in fact what New Yorkers Tom Pritchard and Billy Jarecki (from the Mädderlake firm) take home at the end of the week, when the shop closes. Spontaneous arrangements are very American. Photos of nineteenth-century American interiors already show compositions that juxtapose various recipients and many blooms, as seen in Celia Thaxter's Maine home around 1890 (*top right*).

THE BOLD EXTRAVAGANCE OF ENGLISH FLORISTS

Many European florists also qualify for the fashionable title of "floral designer." They stage-manage the entire design of a reception or party, matching their floral compositions to the color of table linen and china, adjusting the lighting, concocting patios and arbors, and sometimes totally transforming the space they are given. This broader conception of the trade is now more widely accepted everywhere. Unlike the American trend, however, European florists are still florists, which means that they usually keep a shop with a handsome window display. Some shops, for that matter, have become so famous that they are now part of the tourist path. Japanese tourists visiting Paris, for instance, make a point of admiring Lachaume's legendary display. The talented florist Tage Andersen in Copenhagen has so many visitors that he charges a forty-crown entrance fee (reimbursed, apparently, if a purchase is made). Admission is free at Kenneth Turner's shop in London, where his window displays are spectacular. He has won worldwide recognition for his

sheet of mosquito netting) are decorated almost exclusively with tulips, peonies, lisianthus, and larkspur—plus sunflowers. These simple flowers are arranged in little vases set in niches designed expressly by the decorator.

In Texas, meanwhile, local tradition remains faithful to brocade, and to shades of turquoise and mauve; for these highly distinctive interiors, Texans adore fragrant varieties such as lilies, freesias, and roses. In Indiana, the problem is different. The variety of the flower makes little difference; what counts is color, which tends to be jade, cinnabar, or sage green, in order to add some spice to the neutrality of rooms that have become completely beige and white in recent years.

The exact opposite is underway in New England, now experiencing a revival of damask, silks, tapestries, and Victorian furniture, all "pretty and traditional." Bouquets are inspired by cottage-garden compositions, with a lot of hydrangea and some lilies. The feel is somewhat English, somewhat Dutch—very European.

Lady Pulbrook (*above*), the emblematic head of Pulbrook & Gould in London, decided to devoted her life to the flower trade in the 1950s to overcome her grief at the death of her husband, Sir Eustace, a president of Lloyds. In those days, "ladies" did not go into the flower trade. When she began going to Covent Garden every day before dawn, her butler commented, "If her ladyship has to go into trade, I don't know why she can't open a hat shop—no lady buys a hat before ten in the morning." Lady Pulbrook stuck to her guns, and all of London's high society rallied to her. She launched an entire generation of florists, including Kenneth Turner, who long worked for her.

bouquets as well as his interiors. Turner is capable of anything, from creating Venetian costume parties to transforming a ballroom into a cherry orchard or an auditorium into hanging gardens. He even convinced the venerable Claridge's Hotel in London to change itself into a tropical jungle for an evening. The magnificent carpets and luxurious furnishings in the foyer were removed and Turner set up grottoes and rockeries with real waterfalls. The management's anxiety is not hard to imagine. Vines hung down everywhere and mysterious groves were lit by countless candles. The ballroom was even more extraordinary, plunged into the semi-darkness of a starry night, peopled by bamboos on which bunches of strelitzias blossomed.

London hotels are becoming accustomed to the whims of floral designers. One day, the ground floor of the equally venerable Dorchester was transformed into a veritable garden pond, with everything that goes with it, including rank weeds and fish. It apparently took the manager a long time to recover. It was the idea of Lady Pulbrook, who founded Pulbrook and Gould some forty years ago (where, for that matter, Turner cut his teeth).

Pulbrook and Gould contributed a great deal to the revival of a typically English style. It should be mentioned that Rosamund Gould, Susan

Pulbrook's associate, learned the florist's trade at Constance Spry's school. Add to that the personal—and very sure—taste of Lady Pulbrook, who could never stand chrysanthemums, which she found too conventional, nor "florist's" irises, which she found much too stiff. Gypsophila, meanwhile, "gives [her] a turn," as does the color orange. Lady Pulbrook, now eighty, nevertheless became the prime coordinator of social events, from Buckingham Palace to 10 Downing Street, imposing her "good taste" everywhere. Yet she has an inborn instinct for bouquets that display natural grace.

A good number of varieties which had disappeared from Covent Garden by the 1960s were reintroduced by Rosamund Gould and Lady Pulbrook—rococo tulips, hellebores, euphorbia, and old-fashioned roses. They had to go to cottage gardens to find these varieties. They also rehabilitated wild carrot, although the English, who call it "Queen Anne's lace," had never really dropped it.

This modest flower perhaps sums up British floral style—light arrangements in which each flower breathes freely on its stem, reflecting something of a garden bunch even in the most sophisticated versions. This style differs completely from dense French bouquets, where blossom snuggles against blossom.

These days, florists are like set designers—even for films. Simon Lycett, a young English florist, was hired to do the floral arrangements for *Four Weddings and a Funeral*. He worked twenty hours a day for six weeks. In the spirit of the film, he designed a wreath of anemones, roses, and amaryllis for the door of the wedding chapel (*top*), as well as decorating a chair with freesias, cream roses, and orchids (*above*). *Right:* Kenneth Turner's decoration of a banquet hall in a Venetian palace for a costume party.

PARIS:
HAUTE COUTURE BOUQUETS

Paris has always preferred flowers "cheek to cheek"—bouquets are worked in terms of masses, and so dense that the hand can caress them like fabric. Flowers mimic the feel of velvet or the large silk ruffles of magnificent dresses. Haute couture sets the tone, which means that having a leading fashion designer as a faithful client is the ultimate recognition for France's most talented florists. Baptiste became a blue-chip florist the day Pierre Berger walked into his shop. The clear affinities between Sylvain Durif's dazzling bouquets and Castelbajac's clothes allow the two to fly under the same banner. And Didier-Pierre's taste for violent and baroque tones immediately evokes designer Christian Lacroix. Seasonal colors and blooms spring up with every Paris fashion show, and it is florists who benefit. Indeed, Lacroix revived bouquets by pointing them "southward," favoring Spanish tones of saffron and red, as well as armfuls of carnations. Carnations were positively disliked at the time; no one remembers quite why. But it hardly mattered once Lacroix—via his floral designer, Moulié— began strewing his shows with them, placing a carnation on every chair. For his tenth anniversary show, Lacroix added camellias—not white camellias, of course, which Moulié reserves exclusively for Chanel (and which he grows himself to be sure of having enough).

In Paris, then, fashion flowers and fresh flowers come to pretty much the same thing. French florists also draw inspiration, however, from their flower markets. The casual profusion of stalls with their huge, delightful, no-frill bunches has generated a typically French aesthetic. Christian Tortu passionately defends this attitude, claiming that the sight of flowers "should generate the sense of happiness you feel at certain markets." An entire generation of young florists has rallied to this idea of delightful abundance, based on generosity, emotion, things that thrill the eye and speak to the heart. It favors cosy, friendly boutiques where love of flowers is an everyday pleasure. Stores with sophisticated floral displays have become the exception, although the magnificent, spectacular approach is now the specialty of Pierre Declercq (with whom Christian Tortu performed his Parisian apprenticeship). Declercq has bedecked and transformed practically every national monument and palace in Paris. His passion for these settings is wonderfully reflected in his own window displays of grandiose compositions, giant wicker forms, and veritable floral sculptures. Declercq is now unique—everywhere else, small boutiques are springing up, furnished like private, cosy interiors so that customers feel at home.

Although Parisians now like their flowers cosy, the same is not necessarily true of the rest of France. Subtle differences, for that matter, previously existed between one quarter of Paris and another. Rich, formal bouquets from the Right Bank were long distinguishable from the Left Bank's "sprigs and flowerets." Such differences are now diminishing, but there is still a world of difference between Paris and the provinces. In Strasbourg, for instance, Geste-Passion Florists (run by Monsieur and Madame Blumstein, who have earned the award of Finest Artisans of France) respect local tradition by eschewing the "cheek-to-cheek" density of Paris bouquets. Provincial folk from Alsace and elsewhere scarcely appreciate the Parisian "waste" of flowers, considered too dense and too costly. A few blooms suffice, with a lot of foliage for volume. Madame Blumstein fills out her bouquets with rhubarb or iris leaves or, when Christmas comes, boughs of pine and cryptomeria. This marked taste for greenery, in fact, shows that Germany is just across the border.

Parisian florists are known for their small boutiques decorated like a cosy home bursting with flowers. Foreign visitors are often seduced by this approach, exemplified by Marianne Robic's eighteenth-century country home ambiance, Gérard Hillion's armchair-and-tapestry setting, and Atmosphere's tiny garden-shed feel. Mille Feuilles even inhabits a "real" house with weathered furniture, console tables, paintings, and library. *Left:* A bunch of red dahlias lie on a velvet-upholstered armchair in Gérard Hillion's flower shop in Paris.

GERMANY'S SCULPTED BOUQUETS

German florists are not only knowledgeable but highly qualified. Unlike France, England, or the United States, not just anyone can open a flower shop in Germany. A diploma is required, which means that florists are technicians and virtuosos. Their bouquets are complex. An arrangement is no longer whipped up according to mood, but is the result of long reflection, and therefore arrives completely "finished." There is no paper to unwrap, nor should the bouquet be rearranged. No German would dream of tousling, re-organizing, or redoing what is viewed as a work of art. When it comes to artistic creation, the Germans stop at nothing. Thomas Starz, for example, mingles garlands with passementerie (gold thread and pearls) and sets it casually (apparently!) on a rusty old cistern. Or else he places roses in a bird's nest, adorned with a jewel and gold dust. Franz-Josef Wien, meanwhile, does variations on wreaths—a very common motif—in a baroque manner by combining fresh roses and languid clematis with touches of dried, pressed pansies straight out of a herbal. He then adds gold filigree, mother-of-pearl, and colors such as violet

and mauve, plus purple berries with a frosty bloom to lend some drama. The heavily symbolic, allegorical, and coded nature of such compositions can even create an uneasy awareness of the fragility of existence. An example of this is an arrangement by Ursula and Paul Wegener, which places a vase of pale roses in a pond of green water that seems unfathomable and treacherous.

The intellectual approach to flowers is accompanied by technical prowess, a sphere in which Gregor Lersche, spiritual mentor to German florists, is unbeatable. Lersche takes ideas to their limit, such as a bouquet that stands all alone, with no support, no vase, no anything. The artifice remains completely undetectable—an innovation based on the most revolutionary principle possible. But it should not be assumed that Lersche's highly sophisticated compositions are reserved for a small "in" crowd. He proves that originality, strangeness, and the quest for the unusual can also find its place in a bridal posy. Lersche has created some amazing bridal bouquets: a "boomerang" hoop that can be held by the tip of the fingers; a large rosette of gingko leaves skirted in coco fibers; and a royal scepter set with gleaming, gem-like berries and exotic flowers.

Some florists remain aloof from fashion trends. Daniel Ost from Belgium, for example, hates to discuss "trends." Yet Ost is an authentic flower master, respected both in Europe and Japan for successfully striking a perfect balance between Oriental and European floral art. He seems to have been fated to work with flowers—as a small child, he was so keen to pick wild roses growing on a well that he fell in. Miraculously saved from drowning, he acquired a permanent passion for flowers. *Left:* Two arrangements by Ost: a chandelier with orchids, asparagus, and raphia (*top*), and a composition of hydrangea, grasses, and little berries. *Above:* Two "standing" bouquets, eliminating the need for vases, by German florist Gregor Lersch.

AND THE BRIDE'S BOUQUET!

Weddings are big affairs for florists, the occasions they like best. Everything is possible, everything imaginable. There is an infinite number of potential traditions to call on, since weddings incarnate the history of floral habits.

All the floral rituals and customs of yore are perpetuated in wedding ceremonies—garlands are worn, bouquets are carried, men sport boutonnieres, ladies wear corsages. Still more ancient traditions survive in garlands over the church door and along the banquet table, floral arches down the path of the procession, and Roman-style showers of rose petals (some florists sell petals in little packets).

Even the language of flowers, so impoverished these days, returns to the fore at weddings. A bridal bouquet often includes a flower related to the happy couple's first date, or those of their childhood gardens. Sentimental symbolism can sometimes be much more elaborate; the bouquet carried by Alexandra Manley for her 1995 marriage to Prince Joachim of Denmark was an entire discourse in itself. Precise instructions were given to Erik Bering, the famous Copenhagen florist. The composition had to express the union of two worlds, since the Danish prince was marrying a lady from Hong Kong. Thus among the lilies, jasmine, bouvardia, poppies, and roses there was a Bauhenia, the official flower of the great Chinese city. The Dan-

ish royal family also contributed. The Queen had expressly picked myrtle, symbol of innocence and joy, from her garden at Fredensborg castle. The Queen Mother, meanwhile, supplied rosemary as a symbol of eternal love. From Schackenborg castle—the happy couple's new residence—came a few lime leaves. And once the bouquet was composed, two small gold weights were hidden in it, a Chinese symbol of happiness and prosperity.

Brides often want to preserve the memory of these bouquets, which is why florists sometimes advise them to have two identical bouquets prepared. One is carried on the big day, and obviously suffers from all the emotion, heat, and embraces. The other one is left intact, and carefully dried so that it can be preserved under a glass bell, as was once the tradition.

Preserving bridal bouquets has become so common that Karen Young, an English entrepreneur, now devotes herself entirely to the task. Clients send her bouquets from all over the world. Three to five months later, she returns them, pressed under glass and framed. Young also prepares tiny frames for displaying the groom's boutonniere in similar fashion. Once given pride of place in the sitting room, these souvenirs will some day be admired by children (and grandchildren), amazed that their parents were once so young and in love. The bouquets that people offer one another swiftly fade—the most ephemeral of pleasures. Yet since the dawn of time, flowers have offered an eternal promise of happiness.

One of the most fabulous floral decors in recent years was designed for the 1995 London wedding of Prince Pavlos of Greece with Marie-Chantal Miller, a wealthy American heiress. Thirty thousand flowers, including twenty-one thousand roses in eight different varieties, were delivered directly from Holland. This wonderland was orchestrated by Denmark's Erik Bering, florist to the cream of high society. The nave of West London's Greek Orthodox cathedral, Saint Sophia, was decorated with a veritable marquetry of flowers. The composition of the bridal bouquet was nevertheless kept secret until the last moment—it turned out to be an enormous rose composed of hundreds of petals bound together. *Right:* The magnificent flower arrangements in Saint Sophia. *Above:* A wedding cake streaming with roses of sugar created by American confectioner Ann Amernick. *Following pages:* A ball of roses designed to dangle from the bride's wrist, by Au Nom de la Rose in Paris.

Connoisseur's Guide

FLOWERS ADDRESS BOOK

It is obviously difficult to compile a list of all the places where, in Europe, the United States, and Australia one can buy pretty bouquets or find ideas for floral gifts. We have limited ourselves to the most prestigious houses and to those, which by personal choice, we appreciate the most. Furthermore, we have completed the list by adding all the addresses of the establishments mentioned or represented in this book (by indicating the pages in the book one can find the florist's work or name mentioned). This list is moreover restricted and we have without a doubt forgotten some excellent florists that deserve to be on the list. We hope at the very least this guide will help to orientate the reader a little in this abundance of flowers and that it will lead to other discoveries.

FLORISTS

In this summary of the European, American, and Australian florist trade, the most renowned establishments are combined with little local florists, without distinction or hierarchy. We wanted it this way since all of them, in their own way, are professional and at each one of their establishments one will have the pleasure of finding floral decorations styled according to the occasion and mood.

UNITED STATES

(The florists indicated by an asterisk have a shop; the others have floral design studios and can be visited by appointment only)

PHILIP BALOUN
340 West 55th Street
New York, NY
Tel: (212) 307-1675
Philip Baloun's design studio specializes in ball and reception decorations and is one of the most well-known florists in New York. See p. 190.

FLORÉAL *
533 Taylor
San Francisco, CA 94102
Tel: (415) 885-4261
Dominique Pfahl, who is originally from Grasse, France, settled in San Francisco fifteen years ago. There, she created a delightful shop whose style has contributed to the revival of local floristry through her use of garden roses, gathered branches, and country flowers into which Dominique sometimes adds butterflies, and bouquets mixed with lemons and gleaming tomatoes. She particularly excels in her compositions of violets that a local grower supplies her with; she ties them up with ribbons or shows them off in little crowns she creates. She offers "everlasting" violets too (preserved by freeze drying) that she places in simple bunches in little boxes painted by hand. See p. 167.

ROBERT ISABELL
410 West 13th Street
New York, NY
Tel: (212) 645-7767
Robert Isabell, a floral decorator, settled in New York in the seventies, and since then he has decorated weddings and receptions. Among all the flowers he uses, he appreciates above all the perfumed varieties that he skillfully combines to create specific moods. He has, moreover, launched his own line of perfumes that is inspired by the scents of lilies and spring flowers. See p. 190.

MÄDDERLAKE
143 West 21st Street
New York, NY 10011
Tel: (212) 807-9345
Billy Jarecki and Tom Pritchard—who founded Mädderlake more than twenty years ago—like many of their other American colleagues today run a decoration and floral conception consulting business. That means they unfortunately no longer have stores for their customers to visit. Their previous shops, such as the one in Greenwich Village that took all of New York by surprise, were highly decorative: a sort of tropical paradise, endowed with small aquatic gardens and filled in with greenery where dandelions were treated in the same regard as perfumed jasmine or the long stemmed arum lily. In the decors they create today for television or the stage, and in the works they have published, they continue to spread their floral philosophy: the charm of a bouquet rests in the choice of flowers, and the grace of a composition lies in looking artless. See pp. 165, 189, 190.

RONALDO MAIA LTD. *
27 East 67th Street
New York, NY 10021
Tel: (212) 288-1049
Whenever you see a single flower held like a jewel in a ruff of galax leaves or a bouquet in a moss-covered basket you are seeing a design that originated in the imagination of the Brazilian-born New York florist, Ronaldo Maia. When he opened his New York shop in 1968, he was immediately recognized by the press as a remarkable talent and major innovator. He is a master of the classic bouquet or the spectacular party decoration when the occasion calls for it, but many of his distinctive flower presentations are very simple—deceptively so. He has designed party and wedding decorations in Brazil, Costa Rica, Venezuela, and Spain, and has clients all over the United States as well as in South and Central America, England, France, Italy, and Greece.

MARLO FLOWERS *
428A East 75th Street
New York, NY 10021
Tel: (212) 628-2246
Marlo Phillips, a Manhattan florist, is most notably known for her rose arrangements that are very opulent but very simple. She has in particular helped to introduce New York to the style of large rosebuds. See p. 186.

DOROTHY WAKO
Tel: (212) 686-5569
Dorothy Wako is, and for the past ten years has been, one of the most popular floral decorators in New York. She works at all levels, making individual arrangements such as rose baskets imagining festive decor for New York parties, or conceiving floral displays for the Museum of Modern Art. By appointment only. See p. 190.

UNITED KINGDOM

THE FLOWER SHOP
The Heal's Building
196 Tottenham Court Road
W1P 9LD London
Tel: (0171) 636 1666
Julia Hodgkin is one of the most fashionable florists in London and in addition to The Flower Shop, she has created The Flower Van. She is also responsible for buying flowers for the two shops: flowers from Holland and English varieties are her favorites.

THE FLOWER VAN
The Michelin Building
81 Fulham Road
London SW3 6RD
Tel: (0171) 589 1852

If you set up a van to sell flowers in the open air, and go about it in the right way, it quickly becomes one of the most chic addresses in town: that's what Julia Hodgkin (cf. The Flower Shop) did by setting up The Flower Van in front of The Conran Shop.

John Carter is in charge of floral creations ranging from pretty household bouquets to the most sophisticated floral decorations. Most notably, he decorated the recent wedding of Lady Helen Windsor. Many Americans are frequent visitors to the shop.

EDWARD GOODYEAR
45 Brook Street
London W1A 2JQ
Tel: (0171) 629 1508
The Edward Goodyear store, florist of Claridges Hotel, was created in the 1880s, and it was under the reign of Queen Victoria that the shop was granted the "Royal Warrant" title, an award given to purveyors to the crown. Here, the preferred flowers are lilies, roses, tulips, sweet peas, and in general, all the typical English varieties. See p. 176.

LONGMANS
Bath House
Holborn Viaduct
London EC1A 2FD
Tel: (0171) 248 2828
This is one of the oldest shops in London, created in 1896 by Martin Longman. By tradition, it is one of the privileged purveyors of the City, with a clientele essentially consisting of businessmen. In the shop, a team of florists and phone operators are kept extremely busy responding to requests from banks, financial companies, and other companies that work in the Square Mile.
Since 1947, Longmans has supplied the royal family with flowers. And it was here that Princess Diana's wedding bouquet was conceived and realized: a cascade of flowers more than three feet long. See p. 19.

SIMON LYCETT
London SW18
Tel: (0181) 874 1040
Simon Lycett's floral ambitions began when he was seven years old. Today he is one of the most prominent faces of the London flower trade, especially since he created the bouquets and floral decoration for the movie *Four Weddings and a Funeral*. See p. 192.

MOYSES STEVENS
157–158 Sloane Street
London SW1X 9BT
Tel: (0171) 259 9303

An elegant black and gold facade and spectacular windows throughout all four seasons is the face of this venerable shop that was founded in 1876, following the wedding of a certain Lady Moyses to a Mister Stevens. Here, a lot of roses, anemones, ranunculus, and delphiniums are used for romantic and country bouquets and baskets. Moyses Stevens is one of the traditional purveyors to the royal family and has been granted the Royal Warrant. See p. 176.

JANE PACKER - FLOWER STORE
56 James Street
London W1M 5HS
Tel: (0171) 486 5097
Jane Packer made herself a name by supplying the wedding flowers of the Duchess of York. She, herself, likes very simple and natural arrangements. "At home I keep my flowers until they are dead—I think faded petals are romantic," she confides. She has opened several shops in London, has her own school of floral art, and has published several books on bouquets. See p. 171.

JANE PACKER
SCHOOL OF FLOWERS
32–34 New Cavendish Street
London W1M 8BU
Tel: (0171) 935 2135
(see above)

PAULA PRYKE
20 Penton Street
London N1 9PF
Tel: (0171) 837 7336
Paula Pryke blends vivid colors, in a mixture of typical English exoticism and romanticism—such as banana leaves and camellia leaves mixed with a profusion of roses. Her invigorating and very imaginative style have brought her

---

LIFE THROUGH ROSE COLORED GLASSES

The rose, an eternal messenger of love, has always been—of all flowers—the most prized. But for the last ten years, it has been the object of an extraordinary craze. It's to the point where we have seen the appearance of boutiques that are specifically devoted to roses: that is a unique occurrence in the history of the floral trade. Those of the readers, and they are very numerous, who are devotees of the rose, will find here a few addresses to satisfy their passion.

ROSES ONLY
803 Lexington Ave.
New York, New York
Tel: (212) 751-7673
This florist, who has three shops in New York and one in Toronto, only sells, as the name indicates, roses. The shop stocks more than fifty varieties, directly sent from Ecuadorian rose nurseries and sold "by the dozen" because Americans, unlike the French, have no fixed rules concerning the number—odd or even—of flowerheads that comprise a bouquet. See p. 186.

ROSA ROSA
141 East 44th Street
New York, New York
Tel: (212) 681-9770
Another store uniquely devoted to roses. Certainly in New York as in Paris the rose is flattered: Rosa Rosa sells more than 3,000 dozen every week, and its clients never have enough! See p. 186.

AU NOM DE LA ROSE
4 rue de Tournon, 75006 Paris
Tel: (01) 46 34 10 64
The first Au Nom de la Rose boutique was opened five years ago, the result of an idea thought up several years previously by the singer Dany. The idea of a shop selling only roses was an immediate success. The original boutique gave rise to "Au Nom de la Rose - Diffusion" with seven more Paris shops, and others in Angers, Nantes, Lyon, and Montpellier. Today the enterprise's success is clear: 350,000 rose stems sold each year, in forty, mainly perfumed varieties, and produced by many hectares of roses grown in the Var region. The rue de Tournon shop remains the central showroom but all the other shops carry a range of mixed roses (three prices for three stem lengths), heart-shaped rose cushions and petals for table and other decorations. In Paris deliveries are made by liveried grooms. See pp. 186, 198, 200.

AU NOM DE LA ROSE BOUTIQUE
46 rue du Bac, 75007 Paris
Tel: (01) 42 22 22 12
To complement its bouquets of fresh roses the shop sells rose-perfumed beads for scenting linen, rose-shaped and scented soaps, and all kinds of decorative paraphernalia—including rose preserve for a tea-time treat and rose syrup for flavoring champagne.

a clientele of architects and designers. She has collaborated on the decoration of Terence Conran's restaurants. See p. 171.

PULBROOK & GOULD
Liscartan House
127 Sloane Street
London SW1X 9AS
Tel: (0171) 730 0030
The shop was founded forty years ago by the famous Lady Pulbrook who had then just celebrated her eightieth birthday. In the sixties, Pulbrook & Gould revolutionized the English flower trade by reintroducing local, rural, and garden flowers, altogether in the spirit of Constance Spry. Today, this shop, situated in the heart of Victorian Chelsea, continues to offer rare garden flowers even after the season is over. A number of contemporary florists did their apprenticeship in this shop, particularly Kenneth Turner. Pulbrook & Gould has created its own school of floral art. See pp. 191, 192.

THE LADY PULBROOK FLOWER SCHOOL
Liscartan House
127 Sloane Street
London SW1X 9AS
Tel: (0171) 730 0030
(see above)

KENNETH TURNER
125 Mount Street
London W1Y 5HA
Tel: (0171) 355 3880
Spectacular windows (created by Simon Brown) mark the Kenneth Turner shop, presently one of the biggest names in floral decoration. He conceives the most fabulous decorations, transforming receptions into almond orchard trees in blossom, into hanging gardens, or into exotic gardens. He is internationally renowned. In his shop, you will find very pretty arrangements of everlasting roses that are his bestsellers. See pp. 171, 191, 192, 193.

HARPER & TOM'S
13 Elgin Crescent
London W11
Tel: (0171) 792 8510
The creative spirit of this shop, Tom Vach, is a German born in Milan... despite this one might say that in general there is something a little French in this shop, but only in the way in which he places flowers on his doorstep (which is not done very often in England) or uses his flowers in generous and abundant masses. This style obviously pleases the English a lot because

his shop has been granted the Royal Warrant. See pp. 184, 185.

WOODHAMS
60 Ledbury Road
London W11
Tel: (0171) 243 3141
Stephen Woodhams' flamboyant showroom in Notting Hill is reminiscent of a rococo dining room rather than a florist's, with a lot of red velvet, stained glass, and antique lighting. He uses vibrant colors to dramatic effect, which explains why the Royal Opera House commissions him so often.

EVA GUNDERSON
Tel: (0171) 371 1548
It is no surprise that Eva Gunderson's work is so exotic: she is of Scandinavian parentage and grew up in Hawaii. Her work is easily recognizable, being bold, graphic, and very sculptural. For her, shape is the most important consideration. Her flower pots are always wrapped in unusual fabrics, newspaper or anything she can lay her hands on. Fashion houses love her work, especially Chanel and Yves Saint Laurent.

MOLESHILL HOUSE
The Fairmile, Cobham, Surrey
Tel: (01932) 864532
Trained by Constance Spry, Penny Snell started her flower business in 1959. A fanatical gardener, she uses a lot of flowers from her own garden in Surrey, where she lives with several cats, dogs, four children, and "lots of mossy branches." London museums regularly commission her and she is responsible for the weekly displays at the Victoria & Albert Museum.

SOME OTHER LONDON ADDRESSES:

SUSANNA MORRISON
Tel: (01734) 321687

JO LORAINE
Flora Design House
Tel: (0181) 444 0488

ERCOLE MORONI
McQueens
Tel: (0171) 251 5505

NICKY TIBBLES
Wild at Heart
Tel: (0171) 727 3095

MARY JANE VAUGHAN
Fast Flowers
Tel: (0171) 381 6422

AUSTRALIA

KEVIN O'NEILL FLORISTS
119 Toorak Road
South Yarra
Melbourne
Victoria 3141
Tel: (03) 98665776
Arguably Australia's most renowned name in flowers, the business was founded in 1972 and has grown substantially ever since. Kevin O'Neill's distinctive dark green boxes and gold printed signature ribbons announce the arrival of something special in flowers. The elegant marble-floored shop in Toorak Road is home to a staff of about thirty and produces a never-ending flow of arrangements for births, marriages, and any occasion when flowers are sent. Often the most regular request is for the Kevin O'Neill version of a bright, mixed posy containing a vibrant and bold clash of mixed colors and flowers. The firm's reputation as the creator of spectacular decor for weddings, marquee parties, and premier events is unrivaled.

FLOWERS VASETTE
247 Brunswick Street
Fitzroy
Melbourne
Victoria 3065
Tel: (03) 94194988
This firm specializes in tropical and unusual flowers, which are presented with high standards of artistic ability and style. Flowers Vasette prides itself on original ideas, which are inspired by the unusual blooms supplied by their experienced buyer, to create vivid and exotic floral masterpieces to cater for all floral requests, from weddings to barmitzvahs and any special corporate event.

BLOOMEY'S
61–65 Bayswater Road
Kings Cross
Sydney
NSW 2011
Tel: (02) 93601788
Bloomey's specializes in helpful advice at the point of purchase—customers can select their own cut flowers or supply their own containers to be filled at the shop if preferred. Weddings, receptions, and special occasions are designed in close consultation with clients and other event suppliers; home consultations, and arrangements for office reception areas, boardrooms, and commercial entertaining all receive the same personal attention. Phone orders are taken for the Sydney metropolitan area.

THE FLOWER MAN
402 New South Head Road
Double Bay
Sydney NSW 2028
Tel: (02) 932 756 00
Compared with other florists, the Flower Man offers a very extensive range of blooms, as well as an excellent selection of potted plants and orchids. Open 365 days a year the company services many corporate clients, weddings, and large functions. Specializing in floral decors the Flower Man also has many domestic clients.

FRANCE

(The Paris addresses are classified by arrondissement)

GAIGNARD, LUC
13, rue du Bouloi, Paris 75001
Tel: 01 42 21 42 00
Gaignard is suspicious of monotony, monochromy, and white which, he says, "is not a color." Always in search of something new, and after having grown vivid colors for quite a while, he dreams today of subtle unions of rare and refreshing colors such as blues and mauves. He combines nice contrasts of materials: the matte velvets of geraniums, for example, mixed with gleaming foliage. In any case, it is the humor of the moment which counts because this boutique always has surprises, and from one season to the next, everything can change.

LHUILLIER
2, Place Vendôme, Paris 75001
Tel: 01 42 60 52 15 or 01 42 61 66 02
Situated close to all the luxury hotels in Paris, Lhuillier delivers its bouquets to guests of the Ritz, Meurice, and Crillon hotels. But in spite of this prestigious location, this friendly store has the antiquated charm of a small provincial boutique. It grows its own pastoral compositions and is without pretension, offering pretty baskets of flowers interlaced with ivy and mixed with fruits and vegetables.

VERTUMNE
12, rue de la Sourdrière, Paris 75001
Tel: 01 42 86 06 76
Here—for once—the florist does all the work herself. And this boutique, or rather a workshop in this case, is charming because this is not a traditional boutique: nothing is really set out or put on display. Clarisse Béraud works with flowers under the watchful eye of Vertumne—the god of gardens

and the autumn harvest—among the apple crates, bunches of perfumed roses, the tubs of fresh mint, bunches of "black cat" dahlias, or sprays of black-eyed Susans cut from the garden. This shop, which decorates the nearby Museé des arts décoratifs, offers delightful and highly inventive arrangements (a welcome break from the ubiquitous round bouquet): bundled roses in boxes of Desdemona leaves, or vases entirely decorated with voluminous foliage.

LES MILLE FEUILLES
2, rue Rambuteau, Paris 75003
Tel: 01 42 78 32 93
For Pierre Brinon and Philippe Landri, flowers are an important part of the everyday and make up a real way of life. This is because in their boutique—designed as a domestic interior waiting to be decorated—table linen, flatware, antiques, and furniture mix together alongside an abundance of flower arrangements. In this domestic and cozy intimacy, buying a bouquet is a small moment of rare pleasure that one can find by choosing from among the pretty vases and countless decorative objects.

ATMOSPHÈRE
38, rue St.-Antoine, Paris 75004
Tel: 01 42 76 08 08
Christophe, the artist of the store, combines rigor and casualness with success. He is daring and moreover has never hesitated, when he was still located on the Boulevard Beaumarchais, to transform his doorstep—Christmas day—into a beach with fine sand and seashells. This does not stop him from loving French gardens or from trimming and training his asparagus fern into elegant topiaries. In his small boutique, the profusion of flowers and foliage is strictly organized by harmonies of color. All is carefully thought over, but, through the effect of his natural imagination, Christophe gives a crazy charm to all he touches. Bouquets are never made in advance, but are always made to order. See pp. 184, 185, 195.

HILLION, GÉRARD
36, rue Gay-Lussac, Paris 75005
Tel: 01 43 54 13 26
Gérard Hillion, who studied under Tortu, is like his master a connoisseur of luxury and simplicity, but with a bit of added sophistication. Velvet hangings, salon furniture, and stone urns adorn this turn of the century boutique that has kept its original foliage and small colonnaded shop-front. Numer-

ous bouquets bloom in Medicis urns that Gérard Hillion has a particular liking for, and that have, in a way, become the symbol of the boutique. See pp. 194, 195.

TORTU
6, carrefour de l'Odéon, Paris 75006
Tel: 01 43 26 02 56
In opening this boutique in 1985, Christian Tortu launched a rural spirit in Paris and diffused a certain image of happiness, that one can find—as he says—"in certain markets far from the city." A profusion of peonies, lilacs, honeysuckle, forget-me-nots, as well as branches, mosses, and vegetables are what he uses as his floral stock-in-trade. This is the spirit of Tortu that has created so many imitators and which has led the most talented to consider vegetation in general as a kind of decoration in and of itself. Tortu has expressed his love of nature through all sorts of media: collections of vases and ceramics, and magical candles adorned with rose petals. He also deserves the credit for the popularity of pretty shop-windows that, today, bloom everywhere in Paris, but among which his stays one of the prettiest. Every year his Valentine's Day windows are a real event... but one needs to hurry to see them: they are so irresistible that they are all sold out in a few hours. See pp. 167, 171, 188, 195.

BAPTISTE
85, rue Vaneau, Paris 75007
Tel: 01 42 22 82 31
Baptiste just moved premises—but he retains the same splendid and generous abundance of flowers in his new boutique. And he still has, as always, the cast-iron rabbit that Baptiste takes with him wherever he goes; it is his good luck charm and is the symbol of the boutique—charming and unexpected. The apparent spontaneity of his decor and compositions is the result of a high degree of professionalism: by family tradition, Baptiste has always lived among flowers. For the last five years he has enchanted Paris with his bouquets and supplies a prestigious clientele, including Pierre Bergé, who has become an honorary patron of the store. See p. 184.

MARIANNE ROBIC
41, rue de Bourgogne, Paris 75007
Tel: 01 44 18 03 47
In this boutique one can find the elegance and simplicity of country living. Marianne, who likes short stemmed flowers—primroses, mini-jasmines, pansies, or cyclamens—excels in the

composition of miniature bouquets. Marianne creates small arrangements that can be put in the bathroom or on a table in the family room. These little bouquets are also perfect as well for table decorations: they can be placed next to each guest's plate and given to them at the end of the meal. See pp. 184, 185, 195.

MOULIÉ
8, place du Palais-Bourbon, Paris 75007
Tel: 01 45 51 78 43
Henri Moulié comes from the "older" generation of florists who have practically educated all the young practictioners in Paris. He was born into a family of wine growers from Gers, and has the elegant simplicity of a man with strong roots in the land. He has, moreover, never really broken away from this tradition because he is a gardener as well as a florist. M. Moulié is in effect the only florist in Paris to produce directly a large part of what he sells in his shop: a lot of garden roses (that he likes to take care of himself if he has the time), all sorts of hydrangeas whose midnight blue varieties he loves, and beautiful camellias which he uses to decorate—in profusion—the fashion shows at Chanel. M. Moulié collaborates with the world of haute couture: indeed Christian Lacroix comes to him in search of carnations. He is also the supplier of the Palais de l'Elysée (the President's residence in Paris) and for the public celebration of official holidays. All this is done without ostentaion: M. Moulié is one of the most charming florists in the French capital and his flowers are among the most beautiful in Paris. See pp. 1, 6, 184, 195.

RYU KUBOTA
40, boulevard Raspail, Paris 75007
Tel: 01 45 48 00 98
Ryu Kubota is an esteemed master of flowers in Japan. However he chose to settle in Paris in order to learn the western art of bouquets, and since then, he has opened this shop where he offers Japanese-style arrangements that bridge these two floral cultures. He uses a lot of lilies, little arum lilies, and orchids that he arranges in wooden boxes or in sculpted granite vases created for him by an artisan from southwest France. Ryu Kubota is particularly appreciated for his wedding bouquets that are light and airy like blossoming branches which have brought him much success. Since September 1997 the shop also offers floral art classes.

SYLVAIN DURIF
16, avenue George - V, Paris 75008
Tel: 01 40 70 06 01
In this small ocher-hued shop, flower vases bloom in profusion—up to the ceiling, on the stairs, or anywhere they can, in a harmony of brilliant colors. The perfumed touch of vetier roots, jasmine, or violets is everywhere in the boutique. Sylvain Durif, who is one of the most talented florists of his generation, loves all flowers...except for gladioli. See p. 195.

LACHAUME
10, rue Royale, Paris 75008
Tel: 01 42 60 59 74
In a decor of pink marble, rocaille, fountains, and cherubs, the house of Lachaume, created in 1845, is the temple of western floristry for the entire world. And Giuseppina Callegari, who reigns with her children over this venerable institution, continues to uphold the myth. But not everyone who wants to enter may do so. Amateur photographers and people out for a Sunday stroll who constantly stop in front of the store window are turned away. Mme. Callegari takes good care of her establishment, and consequently applies a certain amount of discretion. This is because the clientele here is not ordinary: the guest list proves this, for all the big names in politics, in show business, or art have at one time called at Lachaume. And almost all of them have sat in the "private office" —well hidden behind a velvet door—to write in complete anonymity their messages of sympathy or love. Mme. Callegari affirms that this office has made miracles happen: on one occasion a quickly written message accompanied by a splendid bouquet specially made at the last minute for the occasion (here, the customer's peace of mind is paramount) prevented a separation and even managed to cancel divorce procedures. One must, at least once a year, treat oneself to a big bouquet of violets from Lachaume: they are superb and the staff wil treat you like royalty! See pp. 15, 112, 113, 176, 177, 191.

PIERRE DECLERCQ
83, avenue Kléber, Paris 75016
Tel: 01 45 53 79 21 or 01 45 53 45 56
Whereas Parisian florists often limit their round bouquets to a small, and often cramped, space in their workshops and boutiques, Pierre Declercq thinks big, and has done so for many years. Established thirty years ago on the avenue Kléber, he has always had a passion for doing things on a large scale and adores putting together the craziest

possible projects. All the historic Parisian monuments—la place Vendôme, the Eiffel Tower, the Louvre—have been transformed at one time into exotic palaces or floral gardens by his work. And many fashions and trends were begun by him, such as petal and leaf collages. Another trend was during the Gulf War, when there was a shortage of flowers, during which time Pierre Declercq invented structured bouquets that gave the effect of volume with only a few petals, branches, or bamboo in the bouquet. That is the type of challenge he loves and he is never lacking in inspiration! This artisan, stylist, and sculptor is also the only one to establish an annual collection in the same style as the great couturiers, putting together variations on a given theme using different colors and materials. They go on show in his shop windows at the beginning of August, at the moment when Paris closes down for a month, giving a spectacular indication of the fashions and trends of the months to come. For the 1997–98 season, inspired by the space conquest and Mars exploration, Declerq announced that he will present his flowers in a setting of tires and rubber...interplanetary bouquets one might say! See p. 195.

DIDIER-PIERRE
114, bd Gallieni, 92130
Issy-les-Moulineaux
Tel: 01 46 42 34 00
Didier-Pierre hates neutrality, half finished things, and formal elegance. So much so that, to get away from Parisian conventions and fashion diktats, he moved to Issy-les-Moulineaux a few years ago in order to set up shop in the country. And in this pretty shop leading to a grove of flowering pots and terraced bushes he grows—with energy and extravagance—masses of flowers in all colors.
Oranges and fuchsias, warm browns and blues, roses and reds all go to make generous baroque-style bouquets that are wrapped with raspberry, jade, or gold paper. The total effect is invigorating and lighthearted: the customer reception is one of the strong points of the boutique. See pp. 166, 167, 195.

GESTES PASSION
26, avenue de la Marseillaise
67000 Strasbourg
Tel: 03 88 35 21 28
This famous florist shop in Strasbourg is run by M. and Mme Blumstein who have both been awarded the title of best artisan in France—Monsieur in 1976 and Madame in 1994—a quite exceptional if not unique achievement.

Here, opulent flowers take pride of place, such as the peony and the perfumed varieties from which scented bouquets are created: a handful of lavender, a little bit of mint, some vervain, and citronella. A lot of foliage that Mme Blumstein grows in the garden is added in order to envelop her bouquets with pretty rhubarb or iris leaves. See p. 195.

GERMANY

GREGOR LERSCH
Telegrafenstraße 9
53474 Bad Neuenahr
Tel: 26 41 70 47
For this internationally renowned florist, floral art is not just a job—it is a veritable profession of faith for which, as he says, he "has worked like a missionary" in more than 30 countries. And today, he continues to travel, spreading his "floral philosophy" all around the world, even as far afield as Japan. For Gregor, flowers are eloquent and bouquets have a meaning— "because we need symbols, especially today," he asserts. See pp. 171, 197.

THOMAS STARZ
Blumenladen Inge Hopfensitz
Rosstraße 11
7080 Aalen
Tel: 73 61 61 310
Cornucopias decorated under a veil of gold tulle, birds nests filled with roses, a delicate garland encircled with gold on the bottom of a rusted metal sheet: Thomas Starz, like a lot of his German colleagues, likes to evoke the poetry of flowers, everywhere and especially where we are not expecting it. See p. 197.

URSULA AND PAUL WEGENER
Schaperstraße 19
1000 Berlin 15
Tel: 79 51 52 58
This couple have become symbolic figures in German floristry and an absolute reference for young professionals. Paul and Ursula—at the same time florists, teachers, authors, and photographers—are veritable theorists of their art and have published several books. See p. 197.

JOSEF WIEN
Feldstraße 49
66740 Saarlouis - Lisdorf
Tel: 68 31 49 425
Belonging to a family of gardeners, Josef Wien was brought up around flowers, so that his taste for floral arrangements developed naturally. But, like all German florists, he had to back up this fondness with solid studies: his

approach to floral art was also enriched by his knowledge of music, art, and architecture.
He is defined best—by his own admission—by his use of "historical" settings, from Ancient Egypt to modern times, a technique that he learned with his Swiss and Austrian teachers.

BELGIUM

LES FLEURS ISABELLE DE BACKER
13, rue Royale
1000 Brussels
Tel: 21 17 26 69
This is one of the oldest boutiques in Europe. The historic art nouveau facade, was created in 1895 for the florist Isabelle de Backer who had already established a boutique in Brussels in 1861. She seems to have been the equivalent of France's Lachaume. This house of flowers was at one time converted into a men's clothing store before going back to its original activities. The interior decor was redone fifteen years ago. Now it is decorated with rocaille, mirrors, and fountains. On the other hand, the flowers offer little surprise: one finds, as throughout Belgium, the famous "horoscope bouquets," composed according to the symbolic colors and flowers of your sign. This formula, adopted by several Belgian florists (but which is very fashionable in Germany too), is an enormous popular success.

B. BROOKS FINE FLOWERS
Barbera Brooks, founder and creative director of B. Brooks Fine Flowers has a mission to find and publicize the work of the world's finest florists. Through her guide Fine Flowers by Phone (see bibliography) which lists 240 florists from 27 countries worldwide, all checked out by her team, Brooks aims to take the element of hazard and potential disaster out of ordering flowers for a special occasion. Bringing together creative florists such as Rayon Vert from San Francisco, Paula Pryke, and Ming Veevers Carter from London, and Pure Mädderlake from New York, the guide lists the firms' styles, types of container used, minimum order required and delivery areas.
To order the book or flowers call 888-346-3356.
Website: www.bbrooks.com

DANIEL ÖST
O.L.-Vrouwplein 26
9100 St-Niklaas
Tel: 37 76 17 15
Daniel Öst is beyond fashion. He hates hearing about "floral tendencies," which are, according to him, more commercial than artistic. This is because Öst is an authentic master of floral design, respected in Europe as well as in Japan where he is recognized for having achieved the exact compromise between Asian and Western floral art. His education was unique. As a child, he miraculously survived a fall into a well while trying to gather wild roses. Afterwards, he maintained his passion for flowers despite paternal displeasure and has dedicated his life to flowers after an unhappy love affair. Emotion and feelings remain essential components of his work which he accomplishes however with extreme rigor, even asceticism. His stated aim is "To do the most with the least." And all this without ever using anything other than flowers and elements from nature. The few privileged customers that have the chance to cross the doorstep of his boutique will bring home an armful of treasures, a little parcel of his enchanted work. See pp. 171, 196, 197.

DENMARK

TAGE ANDERSEN
Adelgade 12, DK 1104, Copenhagen
Tel: 33 93 09 13
Tage Andersen has been, for the last thirty years, one of the prominent figures of the contemporary florist trade in Denmark and beyond since his reputation is international. His compositions, always unique and reinvented, halfway between a bouquet and a plant sculpture, have earned him an enthusiastic crowd of admirers, and, because of this, his boutique is one of the most popular in town. His popularity has reached the point where, to protect himself from tourists and curious visitors, he charges an entry fee of forty kroner... which is reimbursed if you prove to be a true lover of flowers—that is to say, if you buy a bouquet of flowers! See pp. 170, 171, 191.

ERIK BERING
Kobmagergade 7, DK 1150,
Copenhagen
Tel: 33 15 26 33 or 33 15 26 11
Erik Bering is the appointed florist to Her Majesty the Queen of Denmark and one of the favorite suppliers of all crowned heads in Europe. He pursued his studies, at the end of the sixties, at Lachaume in

Paris, then in England where he familiarized himself with a romantic and very opulent style that he adopted as his own. His Victorian arrangements and especially his large garlands of roses are unique in their genre. The boutique he occupies today, and since 1972, is one of the prettiest in Copenhagen: it's an old glovemaker's shop, with a glass ceiling painted by hand, and a spiral iron staircase. See pp. 168, 171, 198, 199.

THE NETHERLANDS

GERDA'S
Runstratt 16
1016 Amsterdam
Tel: 20 624 29 12
Gerda van der Berg, whose father was a horticulturist, loves flowers for themselves and brings out their qualities in her very simple and pure compositions. In her boutique, Gerda places Gloriosa petals (a sort of African lily with undulating petals) in little individual tubes that she sticks onto foliage and moss columns. Tulip bouquets let you see their bulbs through the transparency of the vase. Jade green anthuriums are placed by themselves in a large glass cylinder: a simplistic arrangement but one that she repeats several times, obtaining a row of unusual single blooms. See p. 159.

THERA DE GROOT
Cornelis Schuystraat 27
1071 Amsterdam
Tel: 20 662 19 66
This excellent florist proposes a very beautiful choice of flowers, all in a large variety. Her door step is, at the right season, highly decorated and sometimes quite spectacular. You can see on the sidewalk, under the shadow of a large white parasol, gigantic pyramidal bouquets, filled with petals, which could come straight out of a painting by a Flemish master. See p. 156.

MARCEL WOLTERNICK
Naarderstraat 13, 1251 AW Laren
Tel: 35 53 83 909
Marcel Wolternick has become the number one florist in the Netherlands. In Laren, a small pleasant residential city, he grows his own material with an apparent nonchalance. His store, with his shaded courtyard and his sloping roof, gives the impression of being on vacation. On the inside, however, little "conversation" corners—laid out with couches and armchairs—invite the customer to daydream among the palms, asparagus ferns, and citron trees in bloom. Marcel Wolternick is interested in all that decorates life. And his floral compositions—exuberant and natural—are just one of these aspects. He creates floral decorations for the most elegant parties, he organizes rural gatherings and pays attention to the smallest details. He has even composed musical arrangements to orchestrate his vegetal universe in its entirety. See pp. 54, 169, 171, 186.

FLOWER MARKETS

Long before the first flower shops appeared, flower markets already existed and large weekly markets have always offered flower stalls. It's a very old tradition in Europe, and the custom of decorating with market flowers is one of the most popular and pleasant that exists. It is a pleasure of everyday life in a number of European towns, and it is difficult to list every existing market. Here we give a small selection, citing the most famous of them or those we have a habit of frequenting.

UNITED STATES

New York's Flower District is a sidewalk market to be found on Sixth Avenue between West 26th and West 29th Streets. Frequented by the city's florists who come here for the freshest available produce the connoisseur will be entranced by the variety of plants and even trees of every scent and hue.

UNITED KINGDOM

Columbia Road , London E2.
Underground stations: Shoreditch or Old Street.
The small Columbia Road market is open on Sundays from 8 am to 1 pm and it is said that here you can find the prettiest flowers in the English capital. The open air market continues in the tradition of the larger market which once occupied a large Victorian building established by Baroness Burdett Coutts as a counter-attack on what she perceived to be the dishonesty of many cockney market traders. The building was demolished in 1960 but the market continues, and today the place is very colorful and animated with many small displays and street vendors.

FRANCE

THE FLOWER MARKET ON L'ÎLE DE LA CITÉ
place Louis-Lépine, Paris 75004
This permanent flower market is the most famous and oldest in Paris occupying the same area since 1809. By tradition, cut flowers are not usually sold here, but rather flowers in pots and shrubs. Some rare displays are offered as bouquets, however, and in any case nothing is better than strolling along the alleys of these iron pavilions that were built at end of the 19th century. See pp. 92, 146.

THE FLOWER MARKET AT LA MADELEINE, Paris 75008
When this market was created in 1834, it was the most elegant in town and had the reputation for being shamelessly expensive. The horticulturalists came themselves to bring their products, and society ladies did their shopping here. Since then, this market is no longer very picturesque, and reconstruction works have not improved the site. All of the usual products are found here: from fresh flowers to dried ones, and from flowering urns to bouquets of all sorts. See p. 146.

THE FLOWER MARKET AT LA PLACE DES TERNES, Paris 75017
This is the most recent of the three existing flower markets in Paris even though it dates from 1870. In its pavilions—which are not original and lack character—one can find boxed flowers, plants and flowering tubs, all sorts of bouquets, fresh flowers, and dried flowers. See p. 146.

THE FLOWER MARKET AT LE COURS SALEYA, Nice
This is one of the most famous flower markets in France. The writer Colette pays a tribute to it in *Flowers and Fruit* where she is amazed by the violets and mimosas, the "cut branches, holding shiny foliage and tangerines that are laid out along the stalls." The market is open all year, Tuesday through Saturday, and Sunday mornings. See p. 148.

THE NETHERLANDS

THE FLOWER MARKET OF SINGEL, Amsterdam
This market, open every day except Sunday, is situated on the barges on the edge of the Singel canal. It's the place to go and acquire—for a small price—tuberoses, hyacinths, crown imperials, and of course tulips, preferably between 15 April and 15 May. The most interesting, and by far the most beautiful stand, is that of Decorativa; one can also have pretty bouquets made there. See pp. 146, 147, 159.

PROFESSIONAL COVERED AND OPEN MARKETS

Several large cities have a large covered flower market, a large professional center where wholesalers and florists stock up everyday. It is fairly rare—with the exception of the Covent Garden in London—that individuals are allowed to shop there. But, in general, these covered markets are open to the public and even sometimes are the object of guided tours. The reader should be warned though: these Meccas of floral business can be singularly lacking in charm and poetry. However, it is worth going there: on nice days these exceptional concentrations of flowers of all varieties constitute a very interesting and unique spectacle full of color.

NEW COVENT GARDEN, FLOWER MARKET
Nine Elms Lane
London SW8
This flower market, equivalent to the Rungis market in Paris, is reserved to professionals. However, individuals can shop there. One can find treasures from around the world, including pretty daffodils, peonies, and English roses on nice days... on condition that you get there early. See pp. 130, 144, 145, 146, 159, 160, 167, 192.

THE AALSMEER FLOWER AUCTION
(Holland)
A visit to Aalsmeer is certainly not a pastoral walk. This immense covered flower market—the largest in the world—is a continuation of hangars for as far as the eye can see in a bleak Amsterdam suburb. It is, however, unique and fairly amazing. Visitors discover the site from galleries that overhang the incessant traffic of flower carts and the goings and comings of employees who only move by bicycle. One can also see the rooms where the famous electronic dials flash, but one must stay outside, behind the picture window: this is the inner sanctum and no one is permitted to go in (for more information: Bloomenbureau, tel: 31 297 73 45 67). See pp. 142, 154, 155, 156, 159, 163.

ARTIFICIAL FLOWERS

For real flower lovers, the bouquet from a florist or from a market is only one of the thousand and one ways to decorate. Dressmakers and stylists have brought back into fashion the silk, dried, or preserved flowers that a number of shops and artisans now sell. Offered in a wide arrange of dazzling colors, reinvented and reinterpreted, these petals—almost everlasting—have almost as much success today as fresh flowers. In addition to preserved or artificial bouquets, we can add floral paper and fabrics that, by tradition, have always been a favored purveyor of plant-like exuberance. Just as porcelain, ceramic, or even sugared flowers are becoming popular, they offer a *floral art de vivre*.

PORCELAIN AND CERAMIC FLOWERS

MUSÉE DES ARTS DÉCORATIFS SHOP
107, rue de Rivoli
75001 Paris
Tel: 01 42 61 04 02
Here one can find porcelain flowers in the style of the eighteenth-century production at Vincennes and Sèvres. Artisan Didier Gardillou today makes replicas according to traditional methods. To make a single anemone, the countless petals of which must be put together one by one, takes no less than five hours of work. The Museum shop sells some of these delicate creations—whether it be a beautiful peony corolla in full bloom of a floral box, all of Gardillou's creations are unique. See pp. 78, 79.

DRIED AND PRESERVED FLOWERS

Evergreen Designs
Fernside, Fernhill Drive
Whittington, Shropshire SY11 4NF
Tel: (01619) 672825
Karen Young gets requests from all around the world, particularly from newlyweds who send her their wedding bouquet so that she can preserve it. But it is necessary to send her the flowers without much delay—the day after the wedding, if possible. Karen will keep them for about 4 or 5 months to dry them according to natural methods, press them, and faithfully reconstruct the composition under a glass case. She does the same thing with the groom's buttonhole that she places in the same case.

MARTIN ROBINSON FLOWERS
111 Walton Street
London SW3 2HP
Tel: (0171) 581 3702
Here, there are only preserved flowers that Martin Robinson supplies using a provincial producer—roses especially, a lot of roses, arranged in ball-shaped bouquets and arranged in wood or painted sheet metal vases that are specially made for this florist. The Queen is one of his clients and the Sultan of Brunei comes to buy yellow roses from him. See p. 188.

FLORA DESSICA
Crown Piont Farms
Kirby Bedon
Norwich NR14 7DU
Tel: (01508) 470634
In the late seventies Mary Colman teamed up with three friends—Ann Crawshay, Janet Barne, and Sheelin Knolly—to establish Flora Dessica, a business specializing in arranging silk and dried flowers. The team work from a barn at the back of Mary's house in Norfolk. A large part of her garden is used to grow the flowers for Flora Dessica, while the other friends contribute hardy perennials from their own gardens. The company has deliberately remained small, yet much of Flora Dessica's work is for large country houses and stately homes. They have worked for interior designers and their arrangements are ideal for companies and show flats, where having fresh flowers is impractical.

VERDISSIMO, FRANCE
Tel: 04 42 54 92 00
This company, founded in Provence, France, specializes in the production of preserved foliage, bushes, and flowers. In particular it prepares "everlasting" rosebuds used by many florists in their displays and in interior decoration. Just one phone call will bring you Verdissimo's list of the shops in your region which distribute its products. See p. 188.

SUGAR FLOWERS

ANN AMERNICK PASTRY
Washington DC 20815
Tel: (301) 718-0434
Ann Amernick—who created desserts for the White House during Jimmy Carter's presidency—has been perfecting her technique of sugared flowers for the past 20 years. She especially likes pale and creamy roses in button size or spread out whose petals she forms and paints one by one. Then she dries them in the open air on a tray after which she assembles them as you would do with a bouquet of fresh flowers. If you care-

fully take one of her flowers off a cake, you can keep them as a souvenir. Most of her clients are husbands, of course. But she also does a lot of compositions for Valentine's Day and birthdays. A lot of her requests are made a year in advance. See p. 198.

FABRIC FLOWERS

BASIA ZARZYCKA
135 Kings Road, Chelsea
London SW3 4PW
Tel: (0171) 351 7276
Basia Zarzyka's boutique, with its pretty display of multicolored stained glass windows, is one of the most surprising that there is. This fashion stylist conceives quantities of accessories here... all highly decorated: low fronted shoes stitched with silk petals, flowered wide-brimmed hats, giant peonies for extravagant buttonholes. And this is all done in incredible colors: oranges and fuchsias, violets and burning saffrons. It's the house of Guillet in Paris that provides her with a large proportion of the flowers and dyes them specially for her. See p. 183.

GUILLET
99 avenue de la Bourdonnais,
75007 Paris
Tel: 01 45 51 32 98

43 boulevard Henri-IV, 75004 Paris
Tel: 01 42 72 21 94
In 1996 Guillet celebrated its centenary, marking a century of expertise passed on through four generations down to Mme Lubrano-Guillet, the granddaughter of the founder. Today she is the enthusiastic guardian of the family tradition. For, at Guillet, tradition is taken seriously and Mme Lubrano still supplies her father's last client—the Carmelite monastery of Saigon. But tradition has not kept her from overhauling the company's image which at the beginning specialized in flowers for interiors and which is now moving into the world of fashion. This turn has met with great success as proved by contracts with Christian Lacroix, Emanuel Ungaro, and Nina Ricci. Her creations have reached as far afield as Japan where Guillet bouquets are sold by mail order through Nikkei magazine, and where at flower festivals Mme Lubrano is often asked by admirers to sign petals of her beautiful camellias. Guillet products—interior or fashion flowers—are available through the two Paris shops. See pp. 180, 182, 183.

LÉGERON
20 rue des Petits-Champs, 75002 Paris
Tel: 01 42 96 94 89
With its piles of boxes, its wooden counters, and its flights of drawers this work-shop has the feel of an old-fashioned haberdashers' store. Multi-colored buttonholes and sumptuous garlands run riot, arranged in silk paper waiting for the call from the fashionable of *le tout Paris*. They can be attached to combs or hats, or fastened around the neck for prêt-à-porter, or sewn onto fantastic eveing gowns. Some days, by appointment only, M. Légeron receives brides and their mothers to choose and try on the garlands and tiaras for the ceremony. There are also made to measure, often in orange blossom which in order to create the best result must be waxed petal by petal by hand. See pp. 115, 115, 180, 181, 182, 183.

MAISON LEMARIÉ
103, rue du Faubourg Saint-Denis,
75010 Paris
Tel: 01 47 70 02 45
This famous establishment was founded in 1880 by a little feather-maker who was the grandmother of the current M. Lemarié. In this beautiful panelled workshop thirty people create dreams in feather and artificial flowers for prêt-à-porter and haute couture. Here Chanel had her famous camellias made, one of the house specialities which come in several varieties—silk and muslin in black or white, in Rhodoid and even in gold leaf. See pp. 180, 182.

FLOWER FESTIVALS

A celebration or festival without flowers is a rarity. But certain local festivals are entirely consecrated to them. Generally organized around the fine days of the year, they can be the occasion for a pleasant escape to the country. It can happen on a weekend where one will bring back the fragrant memory of a beautiful armful of lavender, a small bunch of violets, or a bouquet of mimosas.

UNITED KINGDOM

CEREMONY OF LILIES AND ROSES,
in London
On May 21, the representatives of Eton College and King's College, Cambridge, both founded by Henry VI, join together for a ceremony at Wakefield Tower, in the Tower of London, on the anniversary of the death of the King. Lilies (from Eton) and roses (from King's) are placed at the spot where the king was executed in 1471.

THE KNOLLYS RED ROSE RENT,
in London
Every 24 June, the representatives of All Hallows by the Tower (one of the oldest religious foundations in London) go to the city hall to offer the mayor a single red rose on a cushion. They continue to pay the property tax of a certain Sir Robert Knollys who, in the fourteenth century, had been ordered to pay this floral tax for having constructed—without municipal authorization—a bridge between two properties on each side of Seething Lane. As he became famous through his warrior bravery, he was only condemned to pay this annual rose...but for life!

THE NETHERLANDS

GREAT FESTIVAL OF FLOWERS
Each year on the first Saturday in September, Holland celebrates its flowers. A big procession of floral floats leaves Aalsmeer for Amsterdam.

THE OPEN GARDEN FESTIVAL
in Amsterdam
Elsbeth van Tets, Keizersgracht 528.
Tel: (31) 20 625 3766
Elsbeth van Tets, an antique dealer and silver expert, had the idea of organizing a festival every weekend in May in which ten beautiful residences in Amsterdam—all of which were built during the time of the West Indies Company—are opened to the public. One can discover the layout of these buildings whose ground floor was originally a merchandise warehouse tradi-

tionally completed with a small garden where the wealthy merchants collected specimens of rare and expensive tulips. These gardens became, in the eighteenth century, extensions of the commercial building but the atmosphere remains and the current owners arrange all sorts of antiques, old fabric, watercolors, or porcelain there during the time of the festival. Elsbeth van Tets herself, living in a beautiful house on the edge of a canal, makes Delft blue and white porcelain tulip vases. The profits of these sales are dedicated to the restoration of the *Hortus botanicus*, the celebrated medicine herb garden created in Amsterdam in 1604. This is an opportunity to step back in time to the Golden Age with the possibility, moreover, of contributing to the upkeep of a horticultural heritage.

SENDING FLOWERS

There are several ways of sending bouquets and messages. The most popular, and in our opinion the surest way, is to go to a favorite florist. You submit your wishes and preferences, you choose the colors, the flowers, and the shape of the bouquet with the florist, and he or she takes care of the rest. If your florist uses an integrated delivery service, you have the certainty that the addressee will receive exactly the bouquet that you chose in the store and that was made there. It is thus the best solution when you have a fixed idea about what you want to give, when you have very precise and very personal demands. Certain professionals are remarkably well organized and send their bouquets all over, without a middleman and within reasonable deadlines.

A number of florists are also affiliated to floral delivery companies. In this case you consult your usual supplier and all of your wishes are taken into account, but the order is transmitted— by phone or internet—to another florist in the neighborhood of your addressee. The second florist carries out your demands and takes care of delivery. This way one avoids long distance travel for the flowers, for example, when one wants to send flowers outside the country. Obviously, in this case, there is the risk that your bouquet will not be, upon arrival, exactly the way you imagined when you sent it. And this is for all kinds of reasons: from one region to another, florists do not use the same supplier, and the flowers available in New York at a certain part of the year might not be available in London or Sydney There can equally well be errors of interpretation even though floral delivery companies are particularly good at solving this problem. This is why Interflora created a catalogue of illustrated references that facilitate the client's choice, and which moreover allows the florist who is in charge of the floral composition to know exactly what he is meant to be doing. It is thus practically impossible that the round bouquet you ordered at your local florist can be turned, at the other end of the country, into a flat bouquet. And if by some chance you do not get what you were expecting, your order receipt allows you to make a complaint. But do not hesitate: the vigilance of the customer is a precious tool for floral delivery companies.

There is also another way to send flowers to our loved ones. This time it does not involve going to the florist, but rather necessitates the making of a simple telephone call, and speaking to an operator who will help you with your choice and note the message to be sent—or, of course, by consulting reference lists and their descriptions on the internet. This service is quick and accurate, but one must not expect miracles: it is impossible—in spite of the variety of proposed choices—to send a floral gift that is personalized. Be that as it may, it is undeniably very convenient if one is in a hurry and in all cases of emergency, from the forgotten birthday that needs to be rectified...to a case of love at first sight!

INTERFLORA

"Your deepest feelings are expressed through Interflora"
To order by phone
(toll free number in the UK):
0800 212 824
(n° vert in France): 0800 20 32 04
Payment by credit card
Interflora has a network of 60,000 florists around the work at its disposal. To send flowers abroad, it is necessary to call the operators that are at your service from 8am to 8pm, Monday through Saturday.
The selection of a bouquet happens in two stages: first you choose from a list the occasion that is closest to your intentions, from first love to engagements and weddings by using "express gifts." Then from the heading that seems the best for the situation, you select one of the proposed floral arrangements. In case of doubt or an elaborate order, for example, it is better to speak with an operator in person.

FTD

(Florist's Transworld Delivery)
To order by phone: 1-800-SEND-FTD
FTD Website: www.ftd.com
Payment by V, MC, AE, Discover, Diner's Club, Carte Blanche
FTD is a floral delivery service that has florists from all over the world at its disposal. All FTD florists maintain a stock of flowers and foliage that pass stringent inspections and thus almost guarantee that the addressee will receive the bouquet you imagined sending. Ordering can be done by phone or on-line, and orders received before 1pm Monday through Friday can be delivered the same day in the US and Canada. Orders placed on Saturday before noon will be delivered the following Monday. FTD even offers a guarantee that reimburses your money or replaces the bouquet within ten days of receiving, as well as a service to remind its faithful clients of upcoming holidays, birthdays, and anniversaries.

WEDDING FLOWERS

Wedding anniversaries are an excellent occasion to send flowers. The symbols associated with these celebrations were probably invented by Americans in the nineteenth century. Among the emblems attached to each year of marriage, one can find, apart from the golden anniversaries, porcelain anniversaries, or pearl anniversaries, some flower anniversaries.

8 years:	poppy
13 years:	lily of the valley
17 years:	rose
46 years:	lavender
51 years:	camellia
57 years:	azalea
63 years:	lilac
66 years:	jasmine

Their useful website allows on-line ordering from their US/Canada and international catalogue, confirmation of order, currency conversion to know the exact price if sending overseas, and a "quotable sentiments" page that suggest what message to send for every imaginable occasion from how to say "I love you" in 100 languages to Valentine's Day and birthday wishes.

1-800-FLOWERS, Inc.
To order by phone: 1-800-FLOWERS
Website: www.1800flowers.com
1-800-FLOWERS is the world's largest florists of one hundred and fifty shops that are company owned or franchised and 2,500 shops that are partners. Partner florists are chosen for their high quality standards, superior customer service and delivery, and their ability to meet 1-800-FLOWERS volume requirements. All 1-800-FLOWERS floral associates are required to participate in the Floraversity, the company's innovative training program

that offers a full range of courses with experienced professors. 1-800-FLOWERS offers a unique range of floral and gift products from Victorian-style arrangements and seasonal floral collections to gift baskets and balloons.
1-800-FLOWERS guarantees the freshness of its floral arrangements for a full week and offers its customers a 100 percent satisfaction guarantee on all products and services. There are approximately 9 million purchases per year through 1-800-FLOWERS stores, toll-free number, and interactive service. The company is committed to educating its customers about flowers in a variety of ways including free educational lectures and design classes at the company's retail stores, newsletters, and reference areas located within the company's on-line stores.

CALYX AND COROLLA
1550 Bryant Street #900
San Francisco
California 94103

To order by phone, 24 hours a day, 7 days a week: 1-800-800-7788
Fax: (415) 626 0134
Calyx and Corolla maintain their reputation for sending only the freshest flowers by having them dispatched directly from the growers by Federal Express. Bouquets are lovingly designed, often wrapped in tissue and bearing handwritten cards with the sender's personal message. An unusual feature is the company's offer of accompanying vases: both bouquets and plants can be ordered complete with carefully chosen vase, basket or cache-pot. They also make edible herb wreaths and table decorations for the stylish cook.

FINE FLOWERS BY PHONE
1236 Spring Street
Saint Helena
California 94574
Tel: (707) 963 4480
Toll Free 888-346-3356
Fax: (707) 963 5240

THE LANGUAGE OF FLOWERS

As a New Year's gift, some florists used to present customers with a calendar that included a "language of flowers." Unfortunately, only a few firms such as Lachaume in Paris still respect this charming custom. In a nod to tradition, below is a brief floral dictionary based on Charlotte de Latour's original *Langage des Fleurs*, published in Paris in 1819 (see pages 102–105). Foreign imitators, as a rule, merely translated the meanings suggested by Latour, but divergences nevertheless emerged, particularly in English-speaking countries. The American symbolism given below is based on the list provided by Phillip's Flowers web site, while British variants [GB] are drawn from an Edwardian language of flowers reprinted by Michael Joseph, Ltd., in 1968. Latour's original French meanings, where they differ, are indicated by [FR]. Readers who dread getting lost in this forest of symbols should simply remember that, in any event, giving a bouquet is an attentive gesture that is always well received.

Acacia: chaste love
Acanthus: the fine arts
Amaranth (Cockscomb): immortality [GB: foppery]

Anemone: forsaken [FR: emotional transport]
Apple blossom: preference
Aster: daintiness [GB: variety, FR: ulterior motives]
Azalea: temperance

B
Basil: hatred
Begonia: beware [GB: dark thoughts]
Box: stoicism
Buttercup: ingratitude [GB: childishness]

C
Cabbage: profit
Camellia (red): you're a flame in my heart [GB: loveliness]
Camellia (white): you're adorable [GB: unpretending excellence]
Carnation (general): fascination [FR: strong, pure love]
Carnation (red): my heart aches for you
Carnation (striped): refusal
Carnation (yellow): you have disappointed me [GB: disdain]
Cherry tree: good education
Chestnut leaf: luxury [FR: do me justice]
Chrysanthemum (red): you're a wonderful friend [GB: I love]

Chrysanthemum (white): truth
Chrysanthemum (yellow): slighted love
Clematis: mental beauty [FR: artifice]
Colchicum: my best days are passed
Columbine: folly
Corn-flower: delicacy
Crocus: cheerfulness [GB: mirth]
Crown imperial: majesty
Cyclamen: resignation and good-bye [GB: diffidence]

D
Daffodil: regard
Dahlia: instability
Daisy: I'll never tell [GB: innocence]
Dandelion: faithfulness [GB and FR: oracle]
Delphinium: lack of seriousness, jest

E
Eglantine: poetry [GB: I wound to heal]

F
Fern: magic [GB: fascination or sincerity; FR: sincerity]
Forget-me-not: true love

G
Geranium (red): stupidity [GB: comforting]
Gladioli: I'm really sincere [GB: strength of character]

H
Hawthorn: hope
Heather: solitude
Holly: defense [GB and FR: foresight]
Honeysuckle: bonds of love
Hyacinth: sport, play
[FR: benevolence]
Hydrangea: heartlessness

I
Iris: faith, hope, wisdom and valor
[GB and FR: message]
Ivy: marriage, fidelity [FR: friendship]

J
Jasmine: amiability
[GB: grace and elegance]
Jonquil: desire [GB: I desire a return of affection]

L
Lavender: distrust
Lilac: first emotions of love
Lily (day): coquetry
Lily (white): purity
Lily (yellow): falsehood, gaiety
Lily-of-the-valley: return of happiness
Lime leaf: conjugal love
Lotus flower: eloquence
[GB: estranged love]

M
Maple leaf: reserve
Marigold: cruelty [GB: grief, despair; FR: sorrow]

Mimosa: sensitiveness
Mistletoe: kiss me [GB: I surmount difficulties]
Myrtle: love, Hebrew emblem of marriage

N
Narcissus: egotism

O
Oak leaf: bravery [FR: hospitality]
Orange flower: chastity
Orchid (cattleya): mature charm

P
Peony: shame or happy marriage
[GB: bashfulness; FR: shame]
Peppermint: warmth of feeling
Periwinkle: pleasant memories
Petunia: resentment
[GB: never despair]
Poppy (red) : pleasure or oblivion
[GB, FR: consolation]
Poppy (white): consolation
[GB: sleep, oblivion]
Primrose: I can't live without you
[GB and FR: early youth]

R
Ranunculus: you are rich in attractions
Rose (leaf): you may hope [FR: I won't press you]
Rose (single, or red): I love you
Rose (white): innocence and purity
[FR: silence]

Rose (yellow): decrease of love, jealousy [FR: infidelity]
Rosebud (white): girlhood
[FR: heart unaware of love]
Rosemary: remembrance
[FR: your presence revives me]

S
Saint John's wort: animosity
Snowdrop: hope [FR: solace]
Stock: bonds of affection
[GB and FR: lasting beauty]
Straw (broken): rupture of a contract
Straw (whole): union
Sweet pea: departure, blissful pleasure

T
Thistle: austerity
Tuberose: dangerous pleasures
[FR: sensuality]
Tulip (variegated): beautiful eyes
Tulip: declaration of love

V
Verbena: enchantment
Veronica: fidelity
Violet (blue): faithfulness
Violet (general): modesty

W
Wheat stalk: riches

Z
Zinnia: thinking of you, in memory of an absent friend

F L O R A L   S A V O I R - F A I R E

Once upon a time floral savoir-faire was governed by all kinds of precepts. A man would never send an ambiguous signal to a married woman by offering her red roses, and a young woman would never accept flowers from someone to whom she was not engaged (nor would she have the temerity to give flowers to a man). These rules were strictly respected until the 1950s, but fell into disuse as taboos were swept away. Some people, however, out of temperament or training, remain attached to a few of the finer points of floral etiquette. When in doubt—and when offering flowers to someone who is not a close friend—it is better to proceed with caution.

FLORAL SUPERSTITIONS
Most superstitions related to specific varieties have fallen out of use—carnations, once considered unlucky, are now wildly popular. Yet some European florists never add carnations to a bouquet without the client's express consent. This precaution is occasionally worth following, especially when it comes to offering flowers to people in the theatrical world. Similarly, violets and pansies should be given only to close acquaintances, since some people still associate them with mourning, which applies all deep-red and purple flowers. Care must also be taken with yellow flowers which, although widely appreciated, retain a very ancient association with infidelity.

GET-WELL AND CONGRATULA-TORY BOUQUETS
When it comes to sending flowers to the hospital or maternity ward, floral savoir-faire is simply a question of common sense. Before sending flowers to a young mother, for example, it is worth verifying that flowers are permitted on the ward (some maternity hospitals forbid them for reasons of hygiene). If flowers are acceptable, then it is always possible to send a fine basket of flowers set in a moistened foam brick, but under no circumstances should a bouquet be offered! Hospitals are not equipped for floral arrangements, and the lack of vases means that a flood of bouquets quickly becomes a burden for everyone. The most reasonable approach—and most polite—is to wait until the mother (or patient) has returned home. That is where flowers are best appreciated.

FLOWERS FOR DINNER
Offering flowers to a dinner hostess is the "thorniest" question of floral savoir-faire. The one golden rule is never arrive with a bunch of flowers, except at the home of close friends. Apart from the fact that the gesture appears somewhat hackneyed, flowers actually make things difficult for the hostess. Just when she is most busy, a

bouquet forces to her drop everything and locate a vase that suits the flowers, arrange them, and find a place to set them. The whole thing becomes more of a chore than a pleasure. Although this problem can be circumvented by having flowers delivered several hours in advance, that is not necessarily the best solution. The hostess has probably organized the floral decoration for the evening, choosing flowers that enhance her table setting. Courtesy obliges her to give your bouquet pride of place, yet chances are that it will clash with everything she has arranged. The third and most elegant option is to send a bouquet of thanks the following day. The hostess will not only be touched, she'll be grateful for all the grief you have spared her.

WEDDING FLOWERS
Rules have fallen by the wayside here, too. All flowers, in every color, are now permitted. Certain traditions survive, however. Thus even though the bride's family no longer necessarily bears the entire expense of floral decoration, the groom still provides the bridal bouquet, which should of course be chosen by the bride herself, since it must match her gown and set the tone for the wedding. Some grooms even buy two bouquets, one to be thrown to the bridesmaids just before the couple leaves on honeymoon, the other—identical—to be preserved.

The groom, his father, best man, and ushers generally wear boutonnieres. The groom's boutonniere might differ slightly from the others (which should all be the same), but should not be any larger. A boutonniere should at any rate be of modest size. Anything bigger than an average-sized rose is too large. A pleasant custom has the groom wear a flower "plucked" from his bride's bouquet. She might even pin it on him herself at the start of the ceremony (assuming that the blooms in her bouquet are not too large).

The couple's mothers and grandmothers can also wear corsages, although this tradition has now fallen somewhat out of fashion, even in the United States where it long held sway.

FLOWERS IN ODD NUMBERS
A French tradition holds that a bouquet should always contain an odd number of blooms. This originally indicated that the bouquet had not been bought at an ordinary market stall, where flowers were always bunched in even numbers. The uneven number therefore became a distinctive sign of a purchase from a florist, where blooms could be chosen one by one. Americans, who have no tradition of street-market flowers, ignore this tradition and the math that goes with it. Given the current vogue for round, dense bouquets, even the French have stopped worrying about the number of blooms, although tradition is still respected when it comes to roses—at a Paris boutique like Au Nom de la Rose, compositions are always based on multiples of eleven stems.

CARE OF BOUQUETS

The charm of flowers reside their fleeting, perishable nature. A bouquet is always a momentary pleasure. That moment can be measured, however: a cut flower has a life expectancy of ten days, which means that a household bouquet should "last" a week, assuming it has been correctly maintained in a vase. Below are some tips gleaned from growers and florists.

The main secret behind bouquets that last concerns the initial freshness of the flowers. Avoid buying flowers on Monday, since cutting and shipping generally come to halt over the weekend, which means that Monday's flowers have spent at least two days in the refrigerator. Ask where they come from—for any given variety, it is always better to choose a local flower, which will have been cut more recently. Look carefully at a flower before buying: its stem should be firm and green, its leaves should show no signs of withering. Buds can be deceptive. When it comes to roses, the bud can be squeezed to verify that it is full and firm. Whatever the flower, make sure the bud has begun to open—tightly closed peony buds, for instance, never open. Multiple buds on a single stem should be three-quarters open.

The first thing to do on returning home, before arranging the bouquet, is to give the flowers water. Place them in a bucket of cold water while still wrapped.

Then prepare the flowers carefully. Remove any leaves below the water line. Leaves degrade and dirty the water, especially stock leaves. Cut the stems at an angle with sharp, clean scissors. The idea is to allow the flowers to absorb the water. Certain florists make the cut under water, to avoid air bubbles getting up the stems and hindering irrigation. Certain varieties profit from having their stems cauterized—place them in hot water for ten to fifteen seconds, then pass them swiftly across a flame. For woody species like lilac, the tip of the stem can be crushed with a hammer, and an inch or two of the bark removed.

As soon as the flowers have been cut, place them in an absolutely clean vase. Be careful of narcissus, which has a sap harmful to other flowers. Narcissus should be placed in its own water for a full day. Then it can be mixed with other varieties, but do not cut the stem again. Avoid over-handling the flowers. They should not be taken out of the vase again. Just add water as needed. Floral additives and nutrient sold by florists may be added if desired—they can be quite effective assuming they are not overused and are suited to the flowers in question (varying qualities of such additives exist).

If the flowers begin to droop, do not hesitate to cut the stems very short. Sometimes they recover their vitality. If all seems lost, take the bouquet and completely submerge it in a bathtub of cold water—the outcome may be disappointing, or it may be surprisingly successful. Tulips, which continue to grow in a vase of water (as do other bulbs), sometimes have stems that droop completely. In this case, roll them tightly in newspaper and submerge them in water entirely. As a rule, the bouquet will straighten.

To revitalize violets, there is no point adding water to the vase. They drink from their blooms, so plunge the entire flower under water.

Finally, place the flowers in a cool room at night. Avoid drafts and direct sunlight at all times, and never place a bouquet near fresh fruit, which gives off ethylene that accelerates the aging of flowers. As every grower knows, a crate of apples in a cold storage room can ruin an entire harvest of flowers.

BIBLIOGRAPHY

WORKS ON THE HISTORY OF FLOWERS AND THEIR USES

The British Museum Book of Flowers, Ann Scott-James, Ray Desmond & Frances Wood, British Museum Publications, London, 1989.

The Elegant Epergne, from the Bunny and Charles Koppelman Coll., Harry N. Abrams, New York, 1995.

Flowers in History, P. Coats, New York, 1970.

Say it with Flowers, "*Don't send a bouquet if you want to be clearly understood*", article by Brent Elliot, in *The Garden*, August 1993, London.

L'Art floral à travers les siècles, Albert Maumené, Paris, 1900.

The Culture of Flowers, Jack Goody, Cambridge University Press, 1993.

L'Empire de Flore, "*Histoire et représentation des fleurs en Europe du XVI au XIX siècle*", collective work, La Renaissance du Livre, Brussels, 1996.

Les Fleurs à Paris, Henry L. Vilmorin, J.B. Baillière & fils, Paris, 1892.

Les Fleurs et les jardins de Paris, Charles Yriarte, Paris, 1893.

Fleurs, fêtes et saisons, Jean-Marie Pelt, Fayard, Paris, 1988.

La Guirlande de Julie, Irène Frain, Robert Laffont, Bibliothèque nationale, 1991.

Histoires de roses, William Wheeler, Ed. du May, 1995.

Recherches sur les couronnes de fleurs, S. Blondel, Ernest Leroux, Paris, 1876.

La Rose et l'Orchidée, "*Les usages sociaux et symboliques des fleurs à Paris au xviiie siècle*", Christine Velut, coll. "Jeunes Talents", Larousse, 1993.

WORKS ON FLOWER PAINTERS

Dutch Flower Painting 1600–1720, Paul Taylor, Yale University Press, New Haven and London, 1995.

Flowers into Art, "*Floral motifs in European painting and decorative arts*", The Hague, Netherlands, Rhodos Publishers and the Kunstindustrimuseet, Copenhagen, Denmark, 1991.

Dictionnaire des peintres de fleurs belges et hollandais nés entre 1750 et 1880, Berko, Knokke Le Zoute, 1995.

Les Fleurs, Peter Mitchell, Scala publications/ Réunion des Musées nationaux, 1993.

Les Peintres de fleurs en France, de Redouté à Redon, Elisabeth Hardouin-Fugier-Etienne Grafe, Les éditions de l'Amateur, Paris, 1992.

La Peinture florale du XVI au XX siècle, collective work, Crédit communal de Bruxelles—Koninklijk Museum voor Schone Kunsten d'Anvers, 1996.

FLORISTS AND FLOWER STYLISTS

An American Style of Flower, Leonard Tharp, Taylor Publishing Company, Dallas, Texas, 1986.

Bridal Flowers, "*Arrangements for a Perfect Wedding*", Maria McBride-Mellinger, Smallwood & Stewart Inc. New York, 1992.

Decorating with Flowers, Maia Ronaldo, text by Denise Otis, Harry N. Abrams, New York, 1978.

Fine Flowers by Phone, Barbera Brooks, Atlantic Monthly Press, 1989.

Jane Packer's New Flower Arranging, Jane Packer, Conran Octopus, London, 1993.

The Floral Decorator, Kenneth Turner, George Weidenfeld & Nicolson Ltd, London.

Floral Style, "*The Art of Arranging Flowers*", Vena Lefferts and John Kelsey, Hugh Lauter Levin Associates Inc., New York, 1996.

Flower Innovations, Paula Pryke, Mitchell Beazley, London, 1995.

Flowers Rediscovered by Mädderlake, Tom Pritchard and Billy Jarecki, Artisan, New York, 1994.

Fresh Flowers, "*Identifying, Selecting, and Arranging*", Charles Marden Fitch, Abbeville Press Publishers, New York, 1992.

Kenneth Turner's Flower Style, George Weidenfeld & Nicolson Ltd, London, 1989, 1994.

Inspired Flower Arrangements, Toshiro Kawase, preface by Miyake, Kodansha International, Tokyo-New York.

Flowers for Four Weddings, Simon Lycett, Ebury Press, London, 1995.

Flower Arranging in the French Style, Pierre Brinon and Philippe Landri, text by Olivier de Vleeschouwer, photos by Christophe Dugied, Flammarion, Paris, 1998.

Mädderlake's Trade Secrets, "*Finding and Arranging Flowers Naturally*", Tom Pritchard and Billy Jarecki, Clarkson Potter/Publishers, New York, 1994.

More Decorating with Flowers, Ronaldo Maia, Harry N. Abrams, New York, 1991, 1995.

Standing Ovations, Gregor Lersch, Gregor Lersch éditions, Bad Neuenahr / Gisèle Blumstein Diffusion, Strasbourg, 1997.

Wedding Flowers, Fiona Barnett, Debbie Patterson, Conran Octopus, London, 1993.

Berings Blomster Verden, Erik Bering, Nyt Nordisk Forlag Arnold Busck, Copenhagen, 1994.

Bouquets, "*Histoire, techniques, composition*", Ursula Wegener, Eugen Ulmer, 1992.

Feuilles et fleurs, Daniel Öst, D. Öst-De Clerck, 1989.

Fleuriste, Christian Tortu, Michel Aveline, 1992.

Florale Meisterwerke in Deutschland, Nob Fukuda, Rikuyo-Sha, Tokyo, 1990.

Vernissage de bouquets de mariées, Gregor Lersch, Appel-Druck Donau-Verlag, Günsburg/ Gisèle Blumstein Diffusion, Strasbourg, 1995.

PICTURE CREDITS

Cover: Christian Sarramon; p. 1 Marc Walter, roses at Moulié; pp. 2–3 Marc Walter; p. 4 The Kobal Collections; p. 6 Photo courtesy of the Norman Rockwell Museum at Stockbridge - Printed by permission of the Norman Rockwell Family Trust © 1957; p. 7 Robert Doisneau - Rapho; p. 8 Fine Art Photographic Library Ltd / Colin Stodgell Fine Art; p. 9 Jacques-Henri Lartigue - Association française pour la diffusion du patrimoine photographique; p. 10 © The Alfred Stieglitz Cat - 1955, By The Metropolitan Museum of Art, N. Y.; p. 11 Rijksmuseum Foundation, Amsterdam; p. 12, P. & M. Maréchaux; p. 13 Alain Soldeville; p. 14 Edouard Boubat - agence Top; p. 15, top, Mary Evans Picture Library - Explorer; bottom, Marc Walter; p. 16 and 17 Serge Fouillet; p. 18 Archive Photos; p. 19 Tim Graham - Sygma; p. 20 The J. Paul Getty Museum, Los Angeles, California; p. 21 Marc Walter / château de la Malmaison; p. 22 The J. Paul Getty Museum, Los Angeles, California; p. 23 The Bridgeman Art Library, Whitford & Hughes, London; p. 24 Marc Walter; p. 25 The Bridgeman Art Library - National Museum of American Art, Smithsonian; p. 26 Scala - Museo Pio-Clementino, Vaticano; p. 27 Edimedia, private collection, detail; p. 28 Marc Walter; p. 29 Osterreichischen Nationalbibliothek; p. 30 The British Library; p. 31 Courtesy of the Trustees of the Victoria and Albert Museum / Brenda Norrish (photo); p. 32 RMN; p. 33 Capella dei Maggi, detail, Quattrone, Florence; p. 34 Marc Walter, flowers at Moulié; p. 35 Scala-Florence, Uffizi; p. 37 RMN; p. 38, top, Albertina Museum, Vienna, D. R.; bottom, Ole Woldbye, Museum of Decorative Arts, Copenhagen; p. 39, top, The Hague Koninklijke Bibliotheek, 74 G 37 a, fol. 1V; bottom, Marc Walter; p. 40 Rijksmuseum, Amsterdam; p. 41, top, Bodleian Library, Oxford, ms Douce 219-20, fol 57 V; bottom, Marc Walter; p. 42 The National Gallery, London; p. 43 Uffizi, Artephot-Bencini; p. 44 The J. Paul Getty Museum, Los Angeles, California; p. 45 Fine Art Photographic Library Ltd & Private Coll.; p. 46 and 47 Munich, Artephot-Artothek; p. 48 *Archdukes Albert and Isabella in a Collector's Cabinet*, detail, The Walters Art Gallery, Baltimore; p. 49 Gilbert Jackson, *A Lady of the Grenville Family with her Son*, detail, Tate Gallery, London; p. 50 Haags Gemeente Museum Collection; p. 51 Frans Hals Museum, Haarlem; p. 52 Musée Boijmans Van Beuningen, Rotter-

dam; p. 53 Fundation Coleccion Thyssen-Bornemisza, Madrid, D.R.; p. 54 Musée du Louvre - Scala; p. 55 Kunsthistoriches Museum, Vienna, Artephot-Nimatallah; p. 56 By kind permission of His Grace the Duke of Westminster OBE TD DL; p. 57 Adriaen van der Spelt and Frans van Mieris, *Trompe-l'Oeil Still Life*, detail, photo 1996, The Art Institute of Chicago, All Rights Reserved; p. 58 Prado Museum, Oronoz-Artephot; p. 59 Rijksmuseum, Amsterdam; p. 60 Edimedia, private collection; p. 61 RMN; p. 62, top, Musée de la Mode and du Textile, coll. Ucad-Ufac, Paris, all rights reserved, photo Laurent Sully Jaulmes; bottom, Rijksmuseum, Amsterdam; p. 63 and 64 top Bibliothèque nationale de France; p. 64, bottom, Musée des Beaux-Arts de Lyon; p. 66, 67 and 68 Rijksmuseum, Amsterdam; p. 69 Andrew W. Mellon Fund, photo Bob Grove, National Gallery of Art, Washington; p. 70 The National Gallery, London; p.71, 72 and 73, Herbier du Muséum d'histoire naturelle de Paris; p. 74 Koninklijk Museum voor Schone Kunsten, Anvers; p. 75 Musées royaux des Beaux-Arts de Belgique; p. 76 Reynolds, *Three Ladies Adorning a Term of Hymen*, detail, Tate Gallery, London; p. 77 Alte Pinakothek, Munich-The Bridgeman Art Library; p. 78 Museo Lazaro Galdiano, Madrid, Oronoz-Artephot : p. 79, Didier Gardillou, photo Marc Walter; p. 80, Musée des Arts décoratifs, Paris - photo Laurent-Sully Jaulmes; p. 81, Schloss Schonbrunn, Vienna - The Bridgeman Art Library; p. 82, Burghley House, Stamford - The Bridgeman Art Library; p. 83 Statens Konstmuseer, Stockholm; p. 84 Marc Walter, private collection; p. 85, Samuel H. Kress coll., photo Richard Carafelli, National Gallery of Art, Washington; p. 86, Det Nationalhistoriske Museum pa Frederiksborg, Hillerod; p. 87 National Gallery of Scotland, Edinburgh, D.R.; p. 88, detail of *Le Billet doux* by Fragonard, The Jules Bache coll., 1949 - by the Metropolitan Museum of Art, N.Y.; p. 89, Photothèque des musées de la Ville de Paris, photo Ph. Ladet; p. 90 coll. Berko, photo Speltdoorn & fils; p. 91 RMN; p. 92, top, Statens Museum for Kunst, Copenhagen, photo Hans Petersen; bottom, Musée des Arts décoratifs, Paris, photo Laurent Sully Jaulmes; p. 93 RMN; p. 94, top, RMN; bottom, Marc Walter; p. 95 château de la Malmaison - Marc Walter; p. 96, Musée des Beaux-Arts de Rouen - Roger Viollet; p. 97 RMN; p. 98, top left, GNAM, coll. Praz, Palazzo Primoli,

photo Vasari, Rome; top right, Fine Art Photographic Library, private collection; bottom right, D.R.; p. 99 Musée des Beaux-Arts de Lyon, photo Basset; p. 100, Musée des Beaux-Arts de Quimper - Giraudon; p. 101 RHS, Lindley Library; p. 102, Bibliothèque des Arts décoratifs, photo J.-L. Charmet; p. 103, background, photo J.-L. Charmet; detail, Martin Breese - Retrograph Archive Ltd; p. 104, background, University Art Museum, University of New Mexico, Albuquerque, D.R.; detail, Marc Walter; p. 105 Coll. des musées de la Ville de Saintes, Michel Garnier; p. 106, top, The Royal Photographic Society, Bath; bottom, The Bridgeman Art Library - private collection; p. 107, *The First of May 1851*, Winterhalter, detail, Royal Collection Enterprises, Windsor Castle - photo A.C. Cooper Ltd. 1993; p. 108, Smith Art Gallery & Museum, Stirling - The Bridgeman Art Library; p. 109 Stern (Art Dealers) Co., London - The Bridgeman Art Library; p. 110 Etude Jean-Claude Anaf & Associé, sale of 8 June 1997, lot no. 122; p. 111 Tate Gallery, London; p. 112 musée Carnavalet, photothèque des musées de la Ville de Paris, photo Briant; p. 113 The Fine Art Society, London - The Bridgeman Art Library; p. 114 top and p. 115, Marc Walter; p. 114 (detail) D.R.; p. 116 D.R.; p. 117 Musée de Nantes - Bulloz; p. 118 Musées royaux des Beaux-Arts de Belgique; p. 119, left, Musée Carnavalet - J.-L. Charmet; details, Fine Art Photographic Library - Findar Macdonnell & Co; p. 120 collection of. M. and Mme Kenber - Marc Walter : p. 121 Musées de la Ville de Paris - Carnavalet - The Bridgeman Art Library - Giraudon; p. 122 courtesy Adam Levene, Albourne - Fine Art Photographic Library; p. 123 City of Bristol Museum & Art Gallery - The Bridgeman Art Library; p. 124 Galerie Berko - Fine Art Photographic Library; p. 125 Fine Art Photographic Library; p. 126, top, Mary Evans Picture Library - Explorer; bottom, D.R.; p. 127 Rheinisches Bildarchiv, Cologne; p. 128 Statens Museum for Kunst, Copenhagen - photo Hans Petersen; p. 129 Gavin Graham Gallery, London, The Bridgeman Art Library; p. 130 Christie's London - The Bridgeman Art Library; p. 131 Museum of London; p. 132 - 133 Richard Green Gallery, London - private collection; p. 134 and 135 Seeberger - Archives photographiques de Paris / CNMHS; p. 136 Musée municipal de Luchon - Dominique Fournier, Eric Le Collen; p. 137, from top to bottom and left to right, Archives photographiques de Paris / CNMHS, Hulton Getty Picture Coll. Ltd, The Bettmann Archive, The Byron Coll / Museum of the City of New York; p. 138 Musée de l'École de Nancy; p. 139 Berry - Hill Galleries; p. 140 Rijksmuseum, Amsterdam; p. 141 Orsay - RMN; p. 142 British Museum, London; p. 143 City of Bristol Museum & Art Gallery - The Bridgeman Art Library; p. 144 and 145, Hulton Getty Picture Coll. Ltd; p. 146 Bonhams, London - The Bridgeman Art Library; p. 147 Marc Walter; p. 148 Zintzmayer; p. 149 Kobal Collection; p. 150 Marc Walter; p. 151, 152, 153, 154 Serge Fouillet; p. 155 Archives of Bloemenveiling Aalsmeer; p. 156 Marc Walter; p. 157 Émile Luiden - Rapho; p. 158 and 159 Marc Walter; p. 160 Hulton Getty Picture Coll. Ltd; p. 161 Doisneau - Rapho; p. 162 Kennet Poulsen; p. 163, 164, 165, 166, 167 Marc Walter; p. 168 Kennet Havgaard - Nyt Nordisk Forlag Arnold Busck; p. 169 Marc Walter; p. 170 Massimo Listri; p. 171 Weidenfeld & Nicolson - Clive Bournsell; p. 172 Royal Horticultural Society, London; p. 173 Royal Horticultural Society, London - Cecil Beaton; p. 174 The Fine Art Society PLC, D.R.; p. 175 Sotheby's - Cecil Beaton; p. 176 Archive Photos; p. 177 (from top to bottom and left to right Marc Walter, Archive Photos; p. 178 Archive Photos; p. 179, top, Archives Interflora; bottom, Archive Photos; p. 180 Archive Photos; p. 181 Marie-Reine Mattera; p. 182 Marc Walter; p. 183 Basia Zarzycka - D.R.; p. 184 Christian Sarramon; p.185 (from top to bottom and left to right) Christian Sarramon, Marc Walter; p. 186 Marc Walter; p. 187 Patrick Jacob - Agence Top; p. 188 Marc Walter; p. 189, top, *Bridal Flowers* by Maria McBride-Mellinger, photo William Stites © 1992 Smallwood & Stewart; bottom, *Decorating with Flowers*, by Denise Otis & Ronaldo Maia, photo Ernst Beadle, Harry N. Abrams Pub, D.R.; p. 190 *Flowers Rediscovered* by Mädderlake, Artisan, a division of Workman publishing, New York, photo John Dugdale : p. 191, top, University of New Hampshire; bottom, Gerhard Stromberg; p. 192 *Flowers for Four Weddings*, Simon Lycett - Ebury Press, photo Sandra Lane; p. 193 John Miller - Weidenfeld & Nicolson; p. 194 Marc Walter; p. 196 Daniel Öst - photo Robert Dewilde; p. 197 *Standing Ovations* by Gregor Lersch, 1997, photo Ralf Hillebrand, Ralf - C. Stradtmann; p. 198 Magazine Victoria, New York; p. 199, Jan Djenner; p. 200 Nicolas Bruant / *Maison & Jardin* - special issue *Mariage* no. 1; p 201 J.-L Charmet.

I N D E X

ACKNOWLEDGMENTS

We would like express our heartfelt thanks to all the florists who helped us and allowed us to profit from their experience: in particular Christophe (Atmosphère) who was the first to guide our research; Didier-Pierre who devoted a lot of his time to us; Gilles Pothier (Moreux Fleurs) whose introductions where invaluable to us; and finally M. Moulié, who showered us with flowers.

We are also grateful to Jean-Claude Anaf (auctioneer), M. Berko, Mme. Blumstein (Gestes-Passion), M. and Mme. Brossard, Véronique de Bruignac (curator of the wallpapers department at the Musée des Arts Décoratifs in Paris), Mme. Callegari (Lachaume), M. and Mme. Coquelin, Mme. de Damas (Interflora), M. Debrie, Mme. Pierre Declercq, Véronique Fontaine (Lambert-Bayard), and Serge Fouillet, thanks to whom we were able to obtain the exclusive photos of floral culture in Columbia, Mme. Jimena Garcon of the Columbian Embassy, Didier Gardillou; Marc Goujard (L'Herbe Verte), Harpers & Tom's, Gérard Hillion, Mr. Jolinon of the Muséum d'histoire naturelle de Paris, M. and Mme. Kenber, Ruy Kubota, Eric Le Collen, M. Légeron, M. Lemarié, Gregor Lersch, M. Longman (Longmans), Mme. Lubrano-Guillet (Guillet), Mme. Mertens (J.-M. Mertens), Daniel Öst, Tom Pritchard (Mädderlake), Pullbrook & Gould, Thomas C. Shaner and the members of the American Institute of Floral Designers of Baltimore, Ms. Ira Silvergleit of the Society of American Florists who collected a large amount of extremely invaluable information, Diana van der Westen of Bloemenveiling of Aalsmeer, Marcel Wolternick, Basia Zarzycka.

The Author would like to thank Ghislaine Bavoillot and all her editorial team, with whom it was a pleasure to work: Nathalie Bailleux, Hélène Boulanger, Soazig Cudennec, Cécile Guillaume, Carine Lefeuvre, Véronique Manssy, and Anne-Laure Mojaïsky.
All my gratitude to Florence Cailly and Hervé Droin.
Finally, and above all, a thousand thanks to Sabine, Corine, and to Marc, of course.

The Publisher is grateful to Mr. John Carter of The Flower Van, Mr. Graham Storey of Moyses Stevens, Mr. Tom Vach of Harpers & Tom's, Mrs. Sonja Wiates of Pullbrook & Gould, and Mrs. Basia Zarzycka for the wonderful welcome in London, as well as the wholesalers we contacted in London: C. Ros from Holland and George A. Moss & Son of Covent Garden Market. Thanks also to Mr. Edouard Carlier of the Beauvilliers restaurant, Mrs. Ariane Dandois, Mr. Rob Demarée of Terra Editions in Holland, Emmanuel Ducamp, Béatrice and Laurent Laroche, Mr. Eric Le Collen, and the Richard Green gallery in London. Finally, we acknowledge with gratitude the entire team who worked on this book: Margherita Mariano, Murielle Vaux, Nathalie Bailleux, Anne-Laure Mojaïsky, Véronique Manssy, Hélène Boulanger, Soazig Cudennec, Aurélie Prissette, Carine Lefeuvre, and Cécile Guillaume.

Library of Congress Cataloging-in-Publication Data
Donzel Catherine.
      [Livre des fleurs. English]
      The book of flowers / Catherine Donzel ; translated from the
French by Deke Dusinberre. -- 1st ed.
            p.   cm.
      Includes bibliographical references and index.
      ISBN 2-08-013655-0
      1. Bouquets.   2. Flowers.   3. Symbolism of flowers.   4. Floral
decorations   I. Title.
SB449.5.B65D6513   1998
745.92--dc21   98-23691